FIRST 50
R&B SONGS

YOU SHOULD PLAY ON THE PIANO

ISBN 978-1-4950-7452-3

7777 W. BLUEMOUND RD. P.O. BOX 13819 MILWAUKEE, WI 53213

Visit Hal Leonard Online at
www.halleonard.com

CONTENTS

AT LAST

Lyric by MACK GORDON
Music by HARRY WARREN

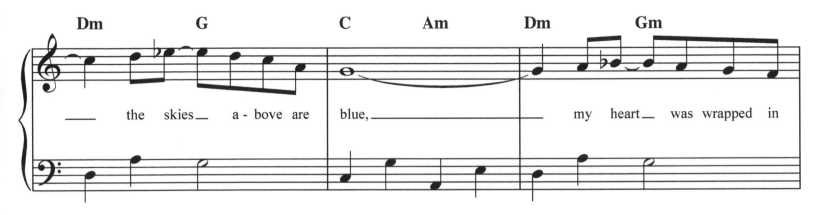

_____ the skies_____ a - bove are blue,_____ my heart_____ was wrapped in

clo - ver_____ the night_____ I looked at you._____

_____ I found a dream that I can speak to_____ a dream that

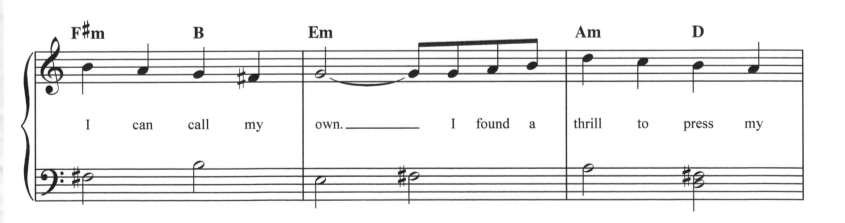

I can call my own._____ I found a thrill to press my

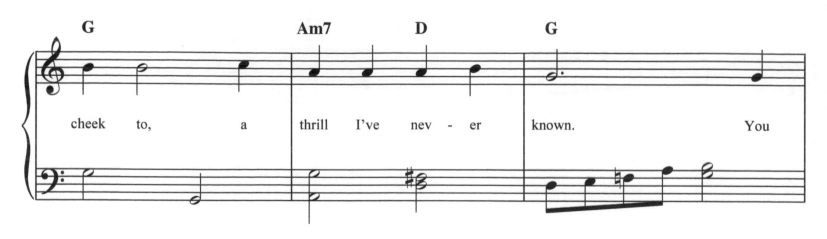

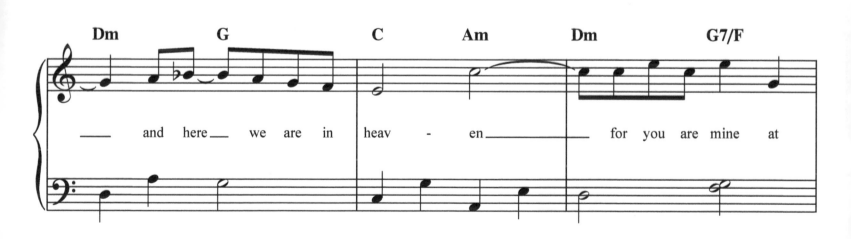

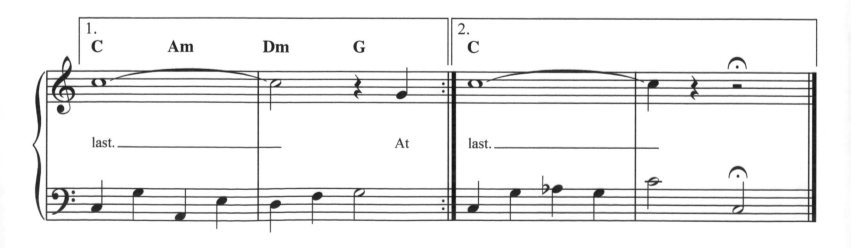

AIN'T NO SUNSHINE

Words and Music by
BILL WITHERS

Slow Rock - Blues feel

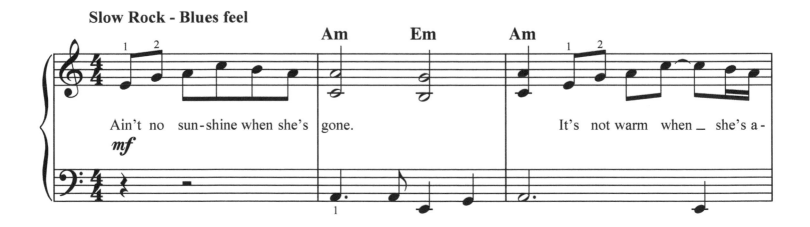

Ain't no sun-shine when she's gone. It's not warm when __ she's a-

way. Ain't no sun-shine when she's gone, and she's al-ways gone too

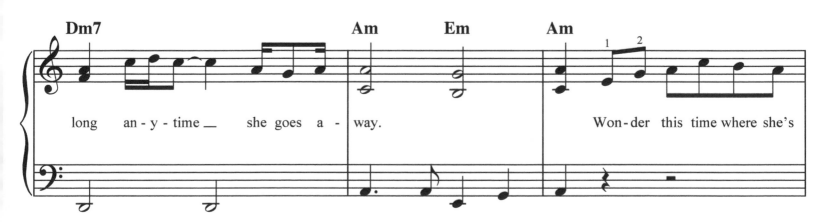

long an-y-time __ she goes a-way. Won-der this time where she's

8

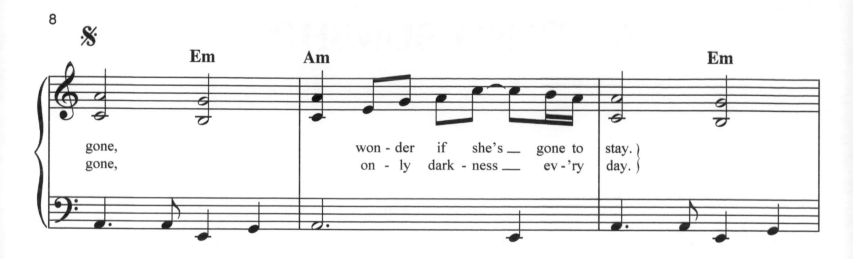

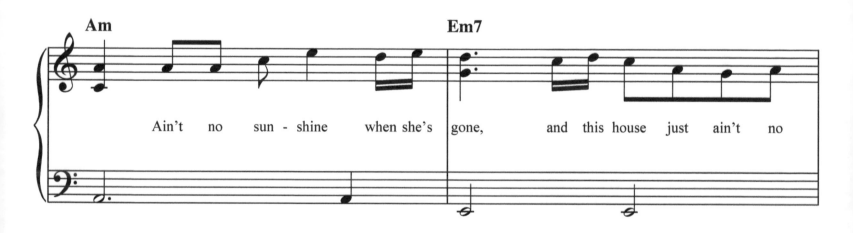

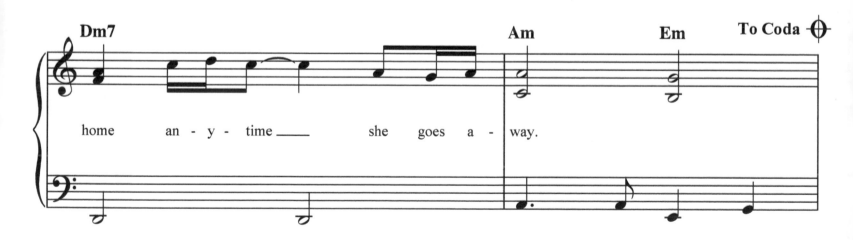

know, I know,_ I know, I know, I know, I know,____ I know, I know, I know, I know, I know,

I know, I know, I know, I know, I know, I know, hey, I ought to leave the young thing a-

D.S. al Coda

lone, but ain't no sun-shine when she's gone. Ain't no sun-shine when she's

CODA

An-y-time_ she goes a-way.

BRICK HOUSE

Words and Music by LIONEL RICHIE,
RONALD LaPREAD, WALTER ORANGE,
MILAN WILLIAMS, THOMAS McCLARY
and WILLIAM KING

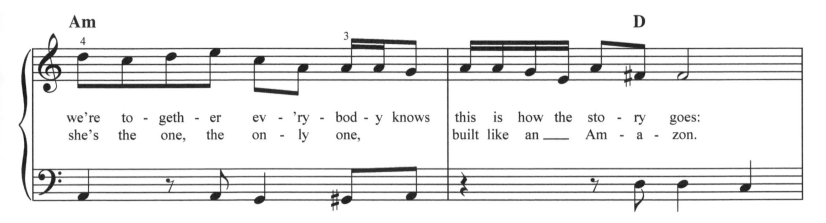

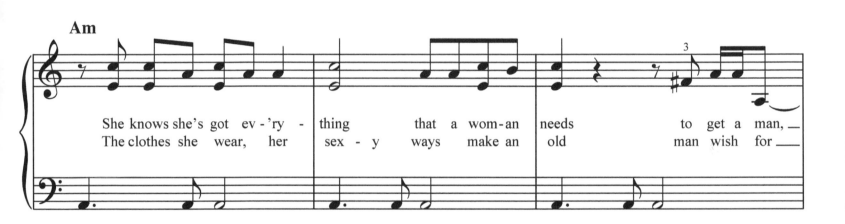

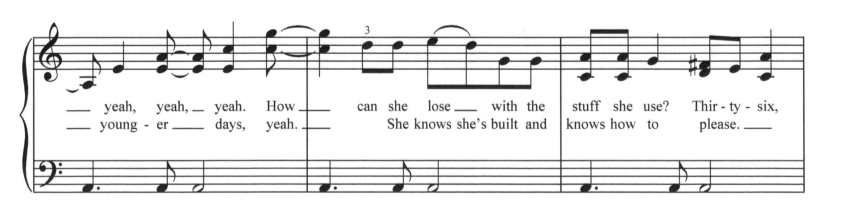

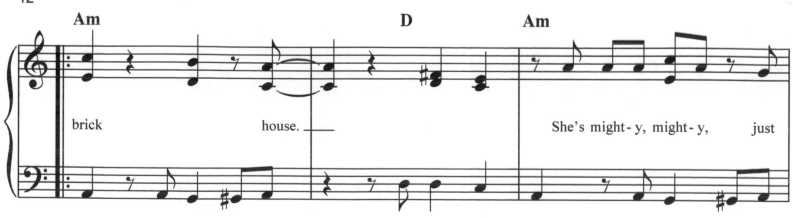

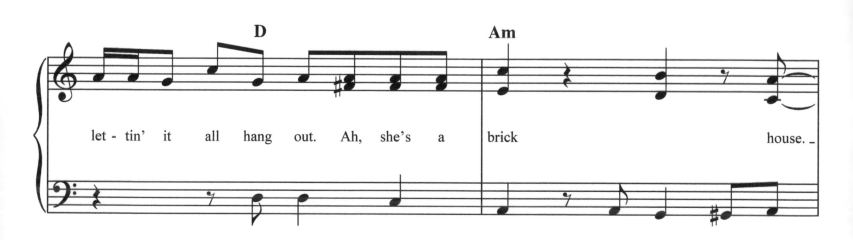

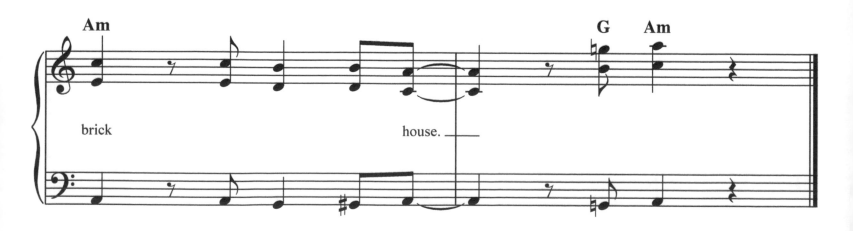

DANCE TO THE MUSIC

Words and Music by
SYLVESTER STEWART

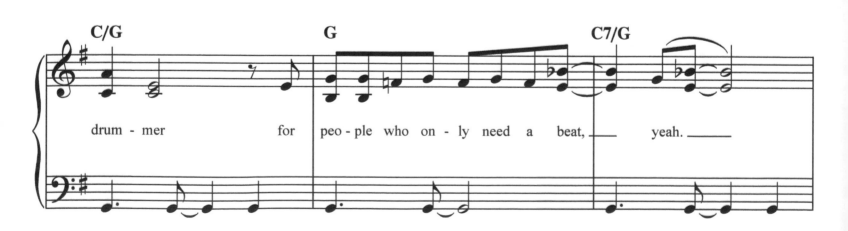

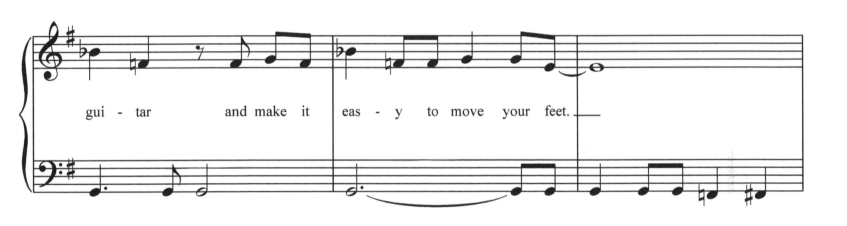

dan - cers   just won't   hide. ___   You   might   like   to   hear ___   my

or - gan.   I   said ___   ride,   Sal - ly,   ride   now.

G7   **C7**   **G7**

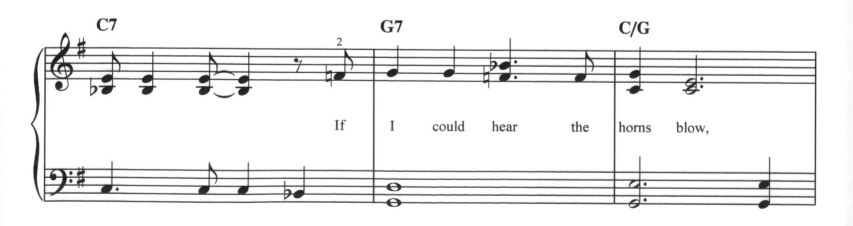

C7   **G7**   **C/G**

If   I   could   hear   the   horns   blow,

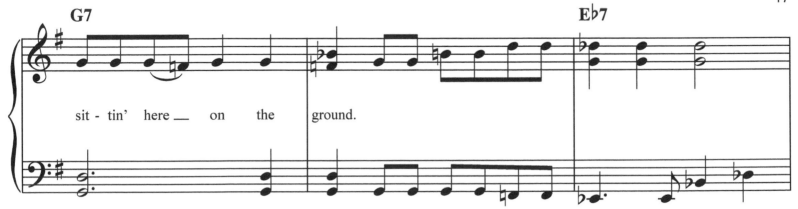

sit - tin' here __ on the ground.

Bum bum bum __ bum bum bum bum bum bum bum bum bum bum __ bum bum

bum bum. bum bum.

EVERYDAY PEOPLE

Words and Music by
SYLVESTER STEWART

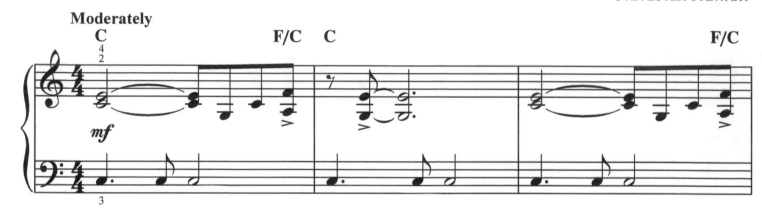

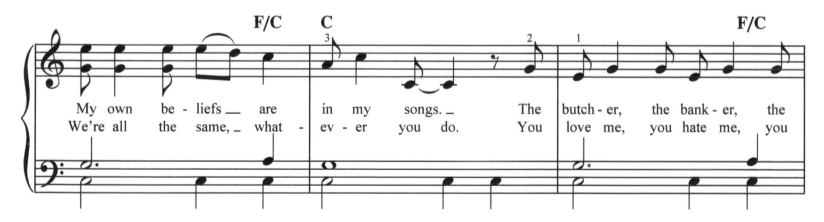

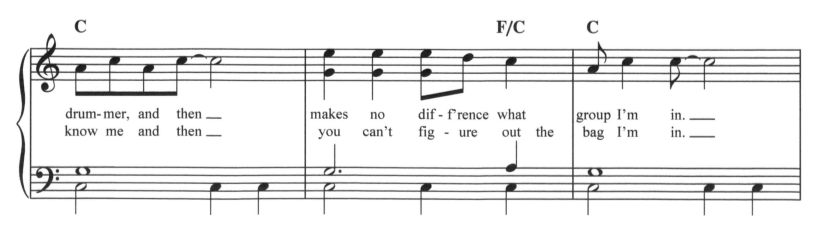

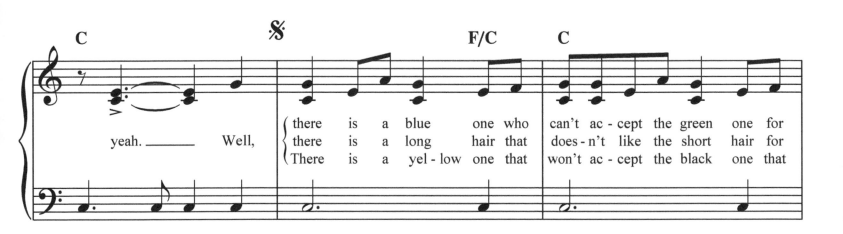

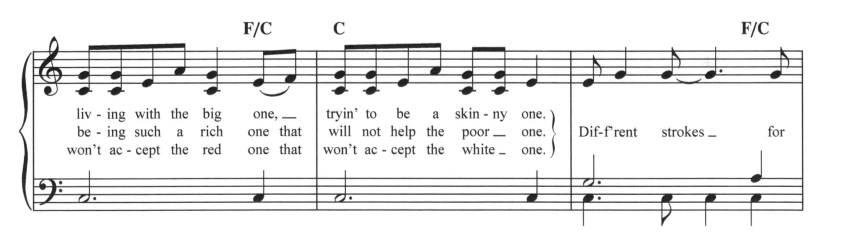

To Coda ⊕
F/C   C   F/C

Ooh, _____ sha sha. _____ We've got to live ___ to -

1. C

2. C   **D.S. al Coda**

geth - er. ___   geth - er. ___

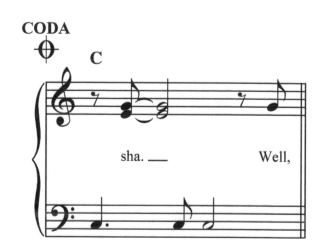

CODA ⊕
C

sha. ___   Well,

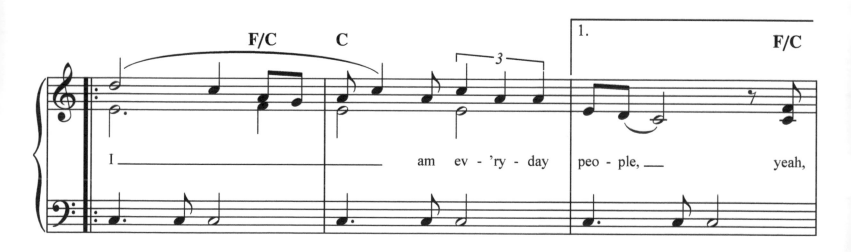

F/C   C   1.   F/C

I _____   am ev - 'ry - day peo - ple, ___   yeah,

C   2.   F/C   C

yeah. _____ Well,   peo - ple. _____

EASY

Words and Music by
LIONEL RICHIE

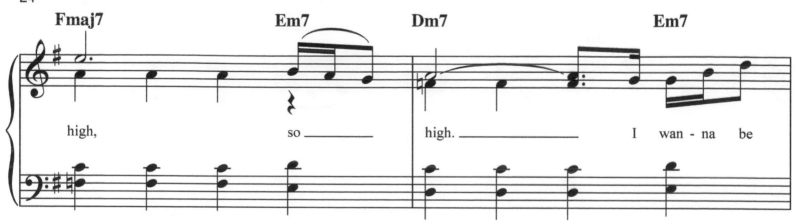

high, so _____ high. _____ I wan-na be

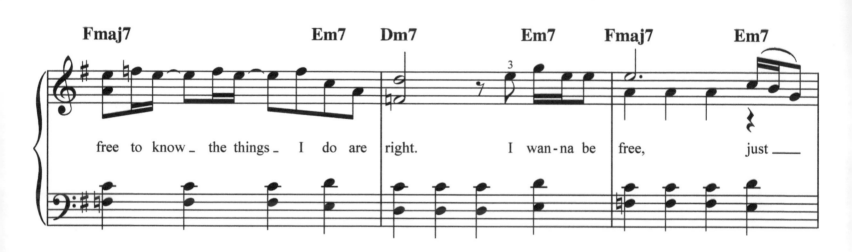

free to know _ the things _ I do are right. I wan-na be free, just ____

me, oh, _____ babe.

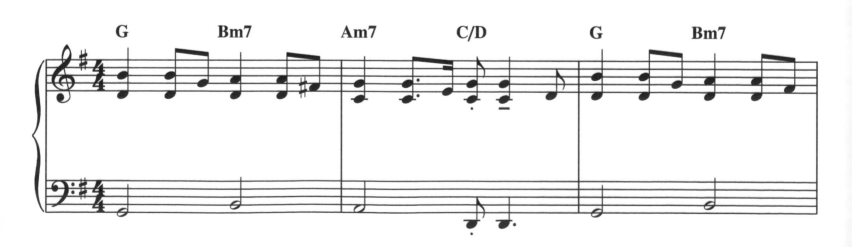

GREEN ONIONS

Written by AL JACKSON, JR.,
LEWIS STEINBERG, BOOKER T. JONES
and STEVE CROPPER

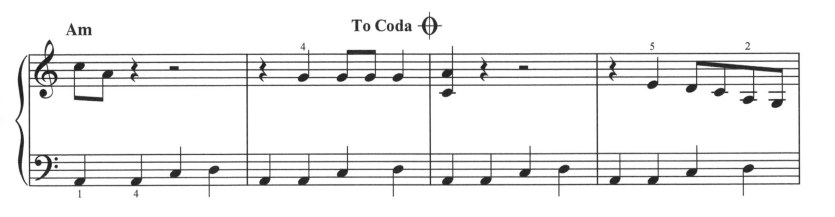

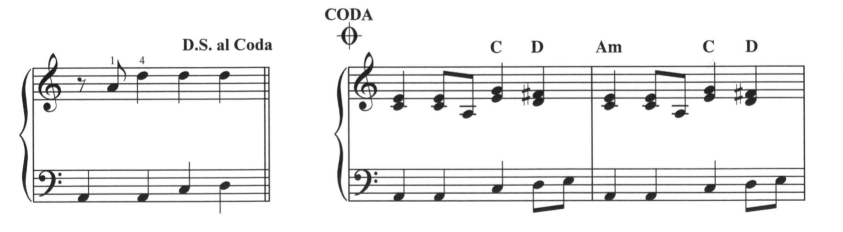

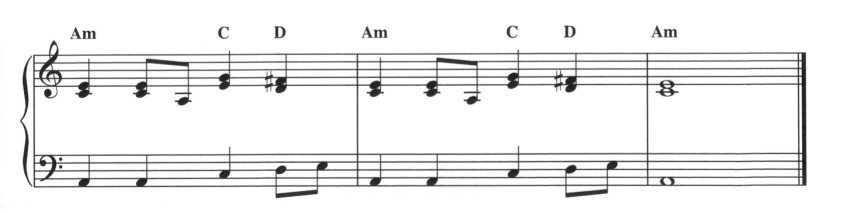

HEATWAVE
(Love Is Like a Heatwave)

Words and Music by EDWARD HOLLAND,
LAMONT DOZIER and BRIAN HOLLAND

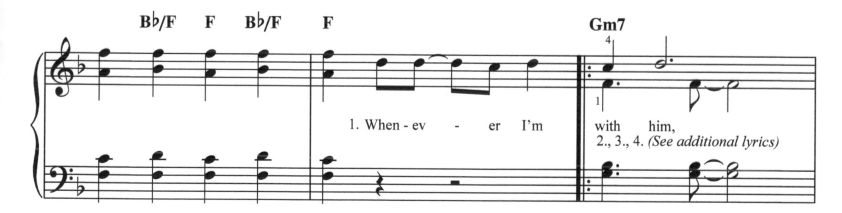

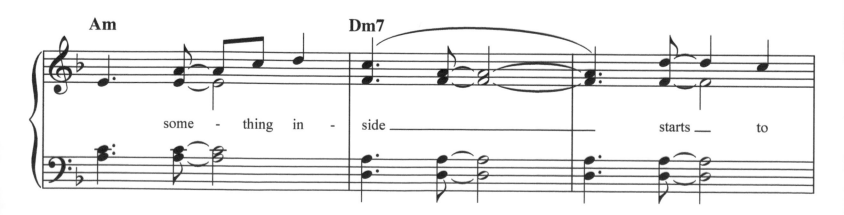

burn - in' _____   and _____ I'm filled with _____ de -

sire. _____   Could it be a dev - il in me _____ or is

this the way _____ love's sup - posed to be? _____ It's like a heat - wave _____

_____ burn - in' in my heart. _____ I can't keep from

cry - in', ___ it's tear - in' me a - part. ___

1., 2., 3. ___ When-ev - er he ___

4.

Additional Lyrics

2. Whenever he calls my name, soft, low, sweet and plain,
   I feel, yeah, yeah, well, I feel that burnin' flame.
   Has high blood pressure got a hold on me
   Or is this the way love's supposed to be?
   It's like a heatwave....

3. Sometimes when I stare in space, tears all over my face,
   I can't explain it, don't understand it. I ain't never felt like this before.
   Now that funny feelin' has me amazed,
   I don't know what to do, my head's in a haze.
   It's like a heatwave....

4. Yeah, yeah, yeah, yeah, yeah, yeah, whoa ho.
   Yeah, yeah, yeah, yeah, ho, yeah.
   Don't pass up this chance;
   This time it's a true romance.
   It's like a heatwave....

I HEARD IT THROUGH THE GRAPEVINE

Words and Music by NORMAN J. WHITFIELD
and BARRETT STRONG

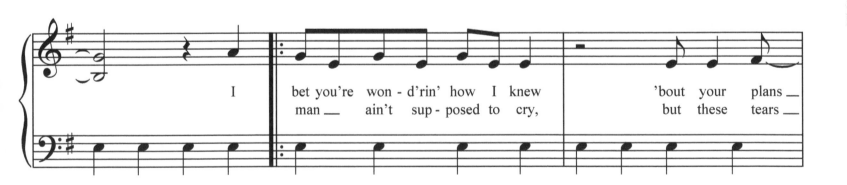

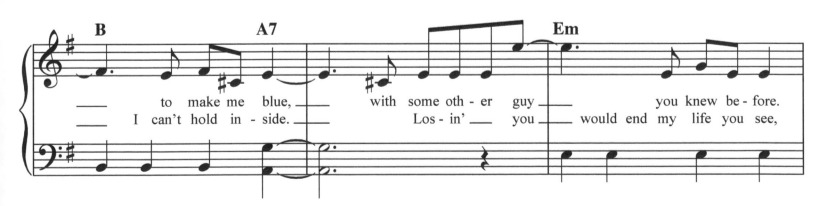

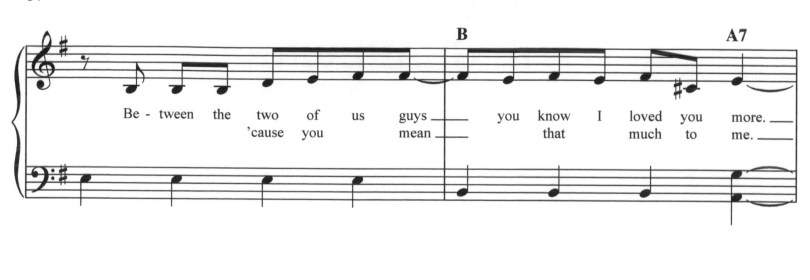

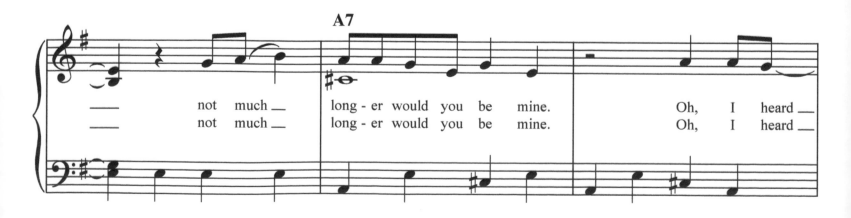

it through the grape - vine. ____ Oh, I'm just a - bout to lose __ my
it through the grape - vine. ____ And I'm just a - bout to lose __ my

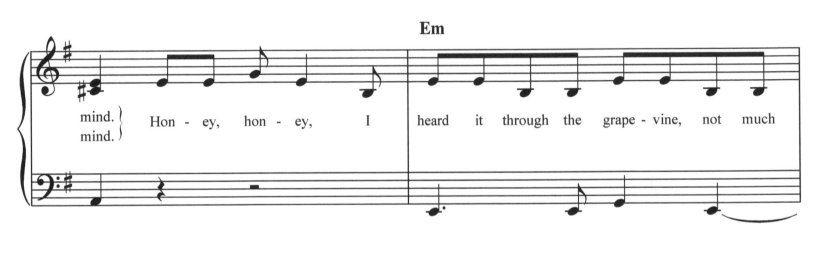

mind. Hon - ey, hon - ey, I heard it through the grape - vine, not much
mind.

long - er would you be mine, ba - by. I know a

HOW SWEET IT IS
(To Be Loved by You)

Words and Music by EDWARD HOLLAND,
LAMONT DOZIER and BRIAN HOLLAND

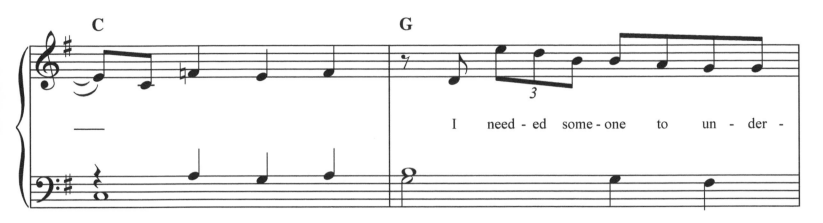

I need-ed some-one to un-der-

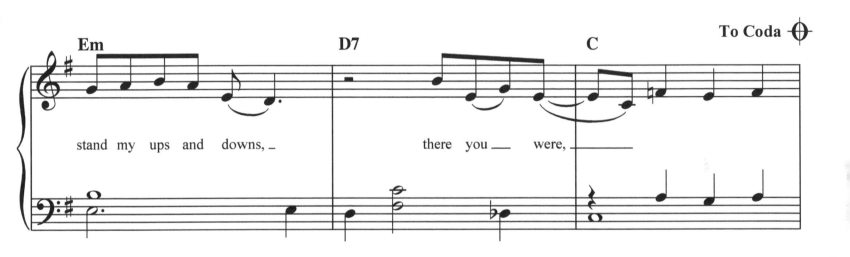

To Coda ⊕

stand my ups and downs, ___ there you ___ were, ___

with sweet love and de - vo - tion,

deep-ly touch-ing my e - mo-tion. I want to stop and thank you,

D.C. al Coda

ba - by; I want to stop and thank you, ba - by.

CODA

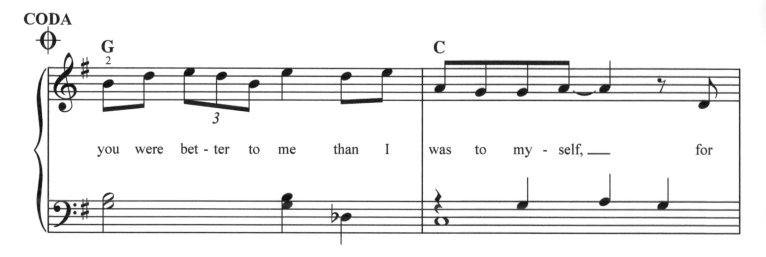

you were bet - ter to me than I was to my - self, ___ for

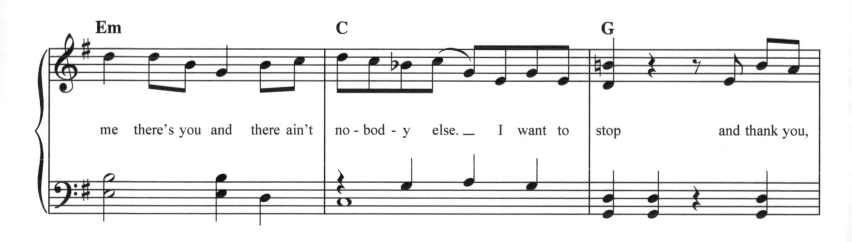

me there's you and there ain't no - bod - y else. ___ I want to stop and thank you,

ba - by; I just want to stop and thank you, ba - by, yes I do.

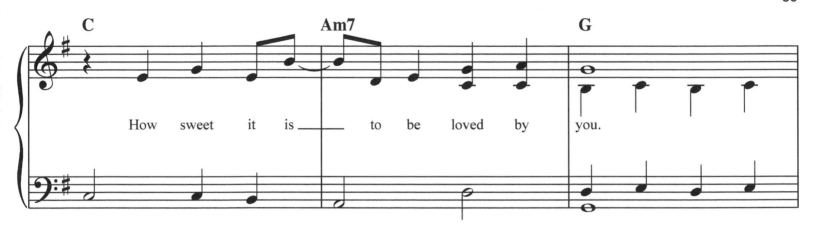

How sweet it is ___ to be loved by you.

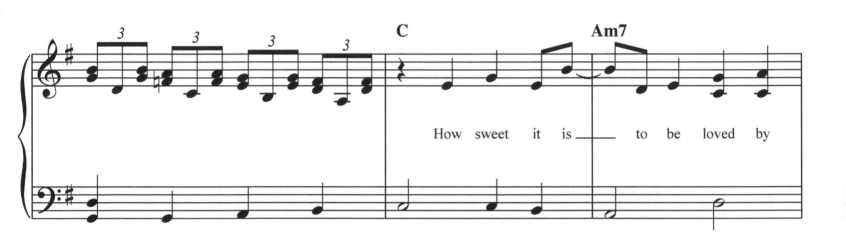

How sweet it is ___ to be loved by

you. How sweet it is ___

___ to be loved by you.

I CAN'T HELP MYSELF
(Sugar Pie, Honey Bunch)

Words and Music by BRIAN HOLLAND,
LAMONT DOZIER and EDWARD HOLLAND JR.

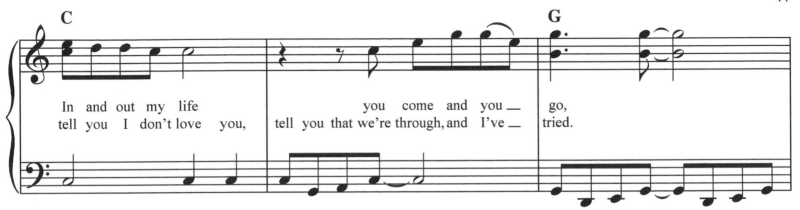

In and out my life
tell you I don't love you,
you come and you go,
tell you that we're through, and I've tried.

leav - ing just your
But ev - 'ry time I
pic - ture be - hind
see your face
and I kissed it a
I get all choked

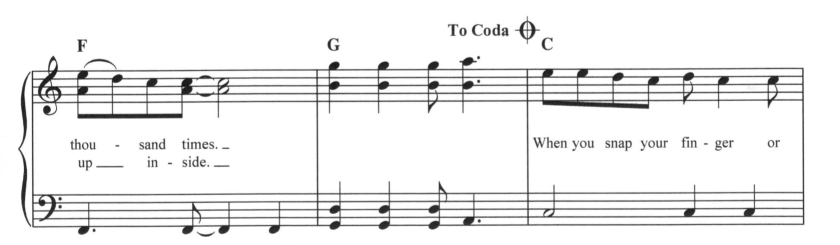

thou - sand times.
up in - side.
When you snap your fin - ger or

wink your eye, I come a - run-ning to you.
I'm tied to your

Dm   **Em**   **F**

a - pron strings _____   and there's noth - ing ___ that   I   can   do. _____

G   **C**   **G**

Dm   **Em**   **F**

Can't   help   my - self,   no, ___ I can't   help   my - self.

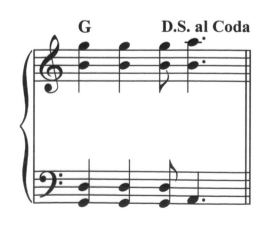

G   **D.S. al Coda**

CODA

C

When   I   call your   name,   girl, ___ it   starts the   flame   burn -

-ing in my heart, tear - ing it a - part. No mat - ter how I try, my love

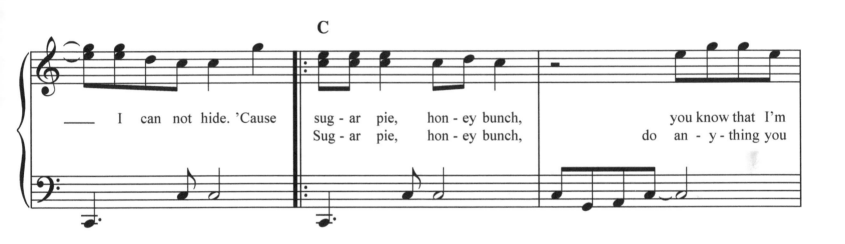

C

___ I can not hide. 'Cause sug - ar pie, hon - ey bunch, you know that I'm
Sug - ar pie, hon - ey bunch, do an - y - thing you

G   **Dm**

weak for you. ___   Can't help my - self,
ask me to. ___   Can't help my - self,

Em   **F**   **G**   **C5**

I love ___ you and no - bod - y else. ___
I want ___ you and no - bod - y else. ___

I GOT YOU
(I Feel Good)

Words and Music by
JAMES BROWN

When I hold — you in my arms, I know that I can do no

wrong. — And when I hold — you in my arms, my

love won't do you no harm. —
love can't do me no harm. —
And I feel — nice.

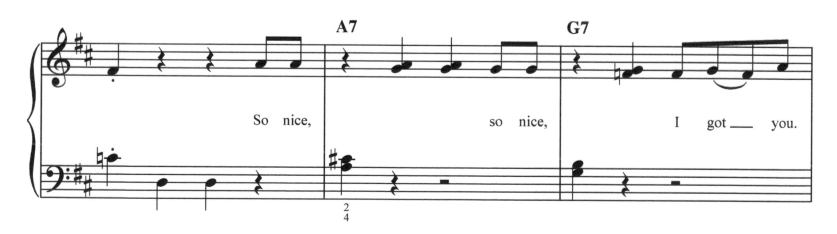

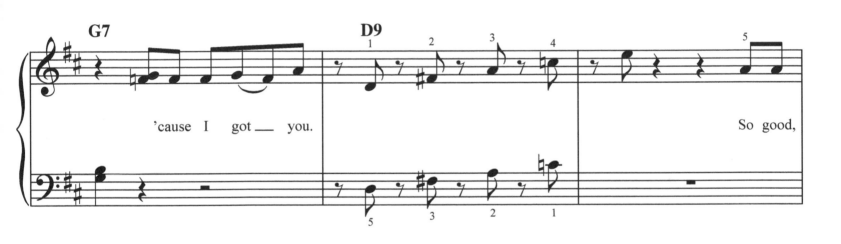

I JUST CALLED TO SAY I LOVE YOU

from THE WOMAN IN RED

Words and Music by
STEVIE WONDER

49

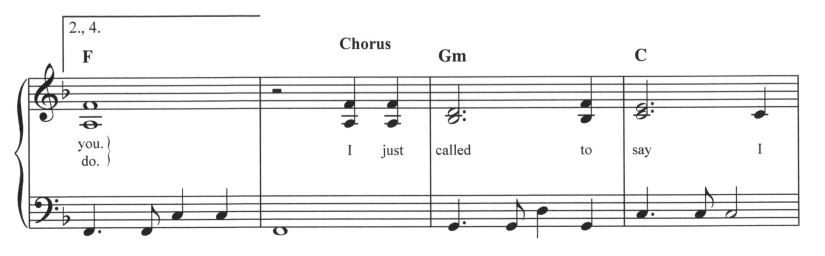

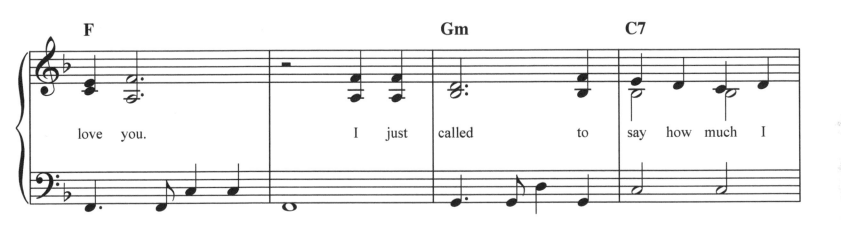

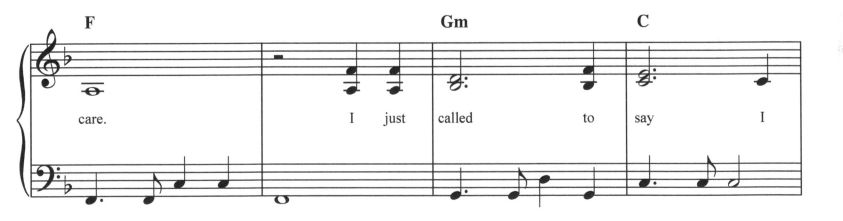

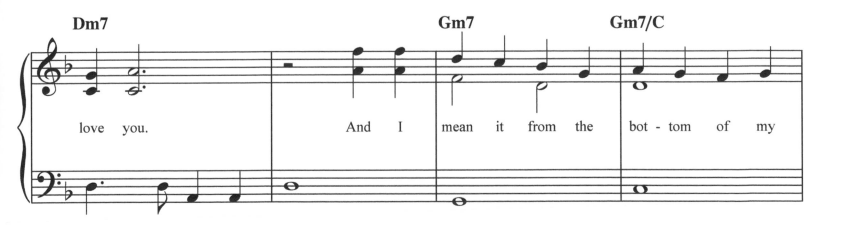

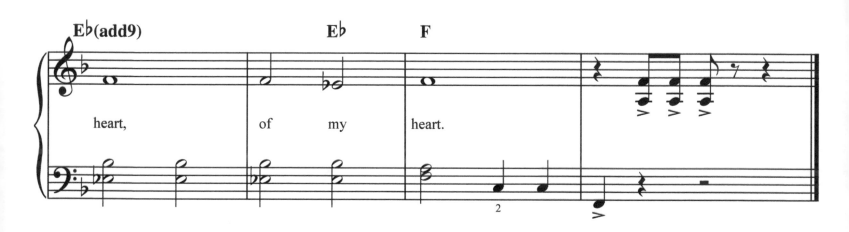

Additional Lyrics

2. No April rain; no flowers bloom;
   No wedding Saturday within the month of June.
   But what it is, is something true,
   Made up of these three words that I must say to you.
   Chorus

3. No summer's high; no warm July;
   No harvest moon to light one tender August night.
   No autumn breeze; no falling leaves;
   Not even time for birds to fly to southern skies.

4. No Libra sun; no Halloween;
   No giving thanks to all the Christmas joy you bring.
   But what it is, though old, so new
   To fill your heart like no three words could ever do.
   Chorus

I'LL BE THERE

Words and Music by BERRY GORDY JR.,
HAL DAVIS, WILLIE HUTCH
and BOB WEST

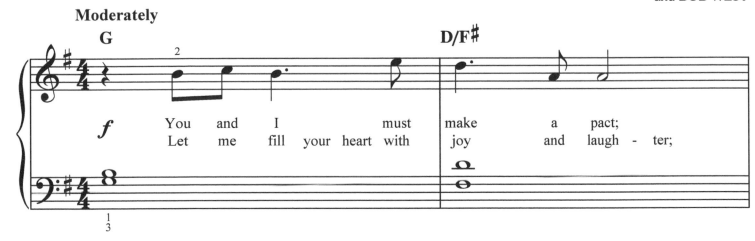

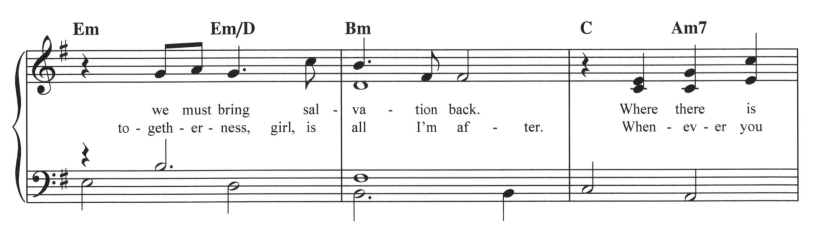

52

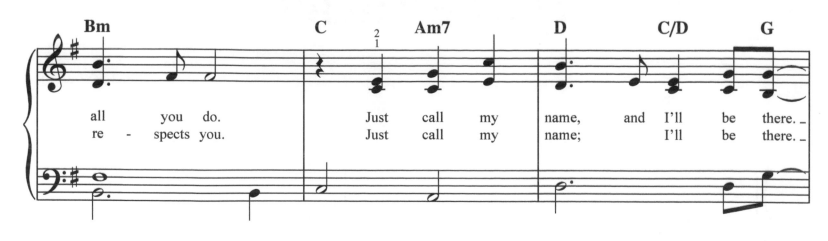

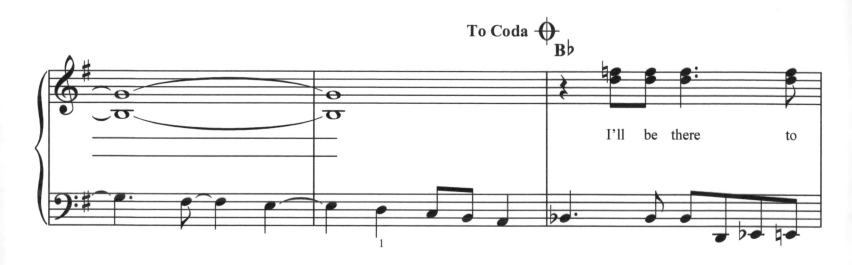

I'VE GOT TO USE MY IMAGINATION

Words and Music by GERRY GOFFIN
and BARRY GOLDBERG

Got to make the best of, of a bad ___ sit - u -

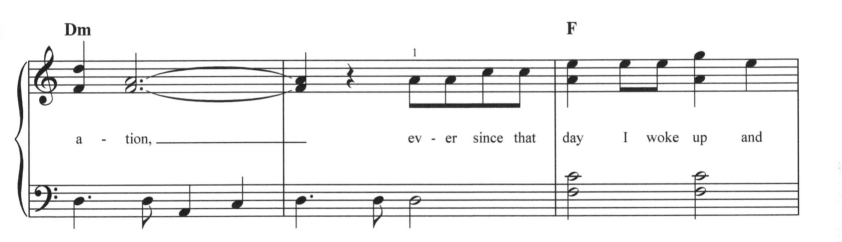

Dm   **F**

a - tion, ___ ev - er since that day I woke up and

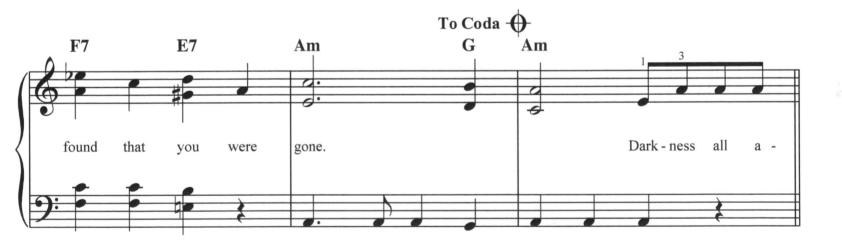

To Coda ⊕

F7   **E7**   **Am**   **G** **Am**

found that you were gone. Dark - ness all a -

round ___ me, ___ black - in' out the sun,

al - i - ty ___ don't do me no good,

Old ___ friends call me but I just don't feel like talkin' to an - y -
'cause our mis - un - der - stand - ing is too well un - der -

one.
stood. Such a sad, ___ sad ___ sea - son
Emp - ti - ness has found me

and it just won't let me go. I go right on
when a good love dies. ___ Not a day ___ goes ___

liv - in' but why I just don't know. ___
by when I don't re - al - ize:

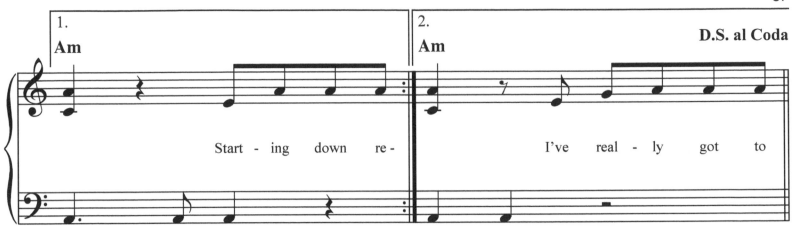

D.S. al Coda

1. Am
Start - ing down re -

2. Am
I've real - ly got to

CODA
Am
G

Am
G Am

G Am

IF YOU DON'T KNOW ME BY NOW

Words and Music by KENNETH GAMBLE
and LEON HUFF

59

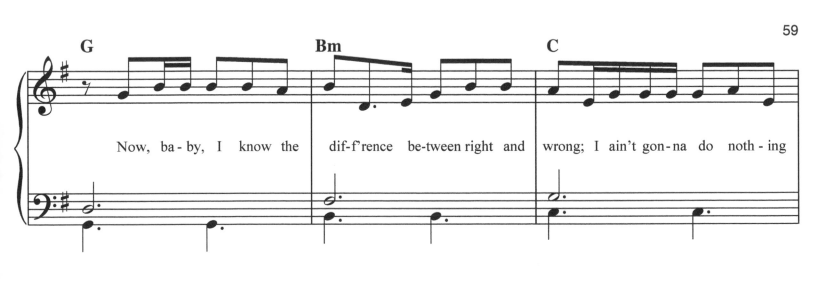

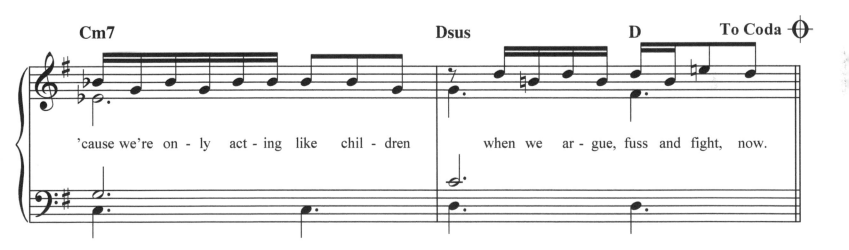

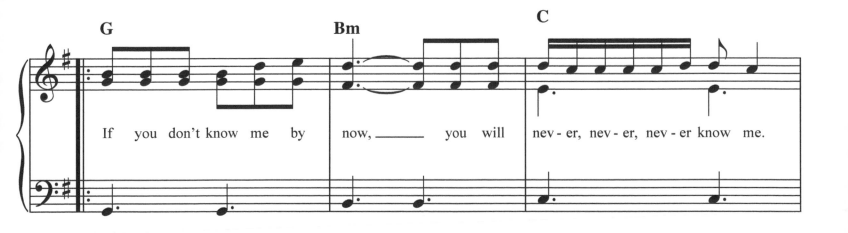

Additional Lyrics

2. We all got our funny moods;
   I've got mine; woman, you've got yours, too.
   Just trust in me like I trust in you,
   As long as we've been together that should be easy to do.
   Just get yourself together or we might as well say goodbye.
   What good is a love affair when you can't see eye to eye?

IF YOU THINK YOU'RE LONELY NOW

Words and Music by BOBBY WOMACK,
PATRICK MOTEN and SANDRA SULLY

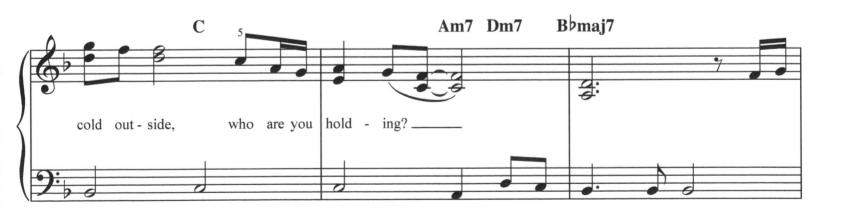

(Spoken:) You know if you all don't mind, I'd like to tell you about this woman of mine.

She's always complainin' 'bout me never bein' at home, but when I'm there, I'm broke. She's

tellin' me 'bout things that her girlfriends got; what she ain't, got, and she wants me to go out and get 'em for her,

(Sung:) but girl, I can't be in two plac-es at one time. _____ If you

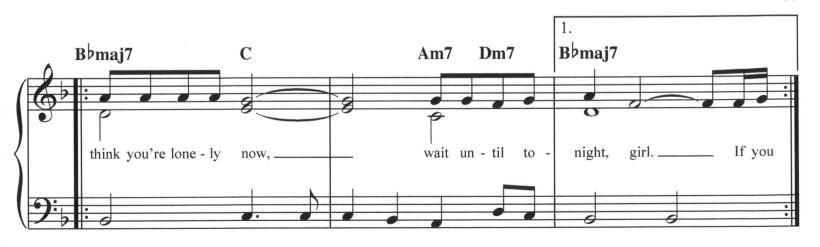

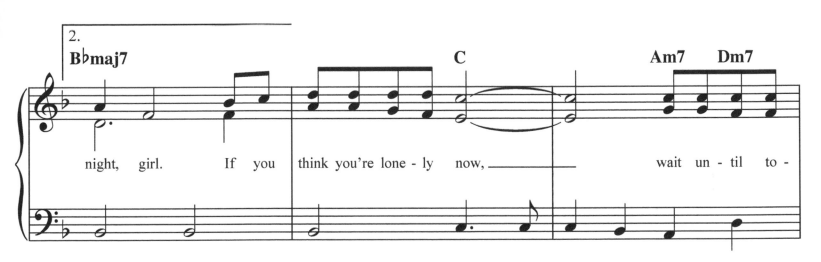

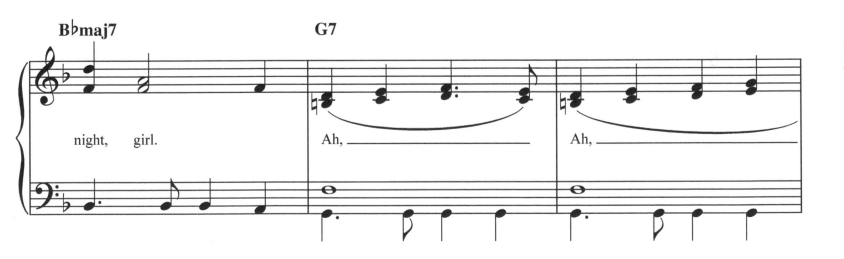

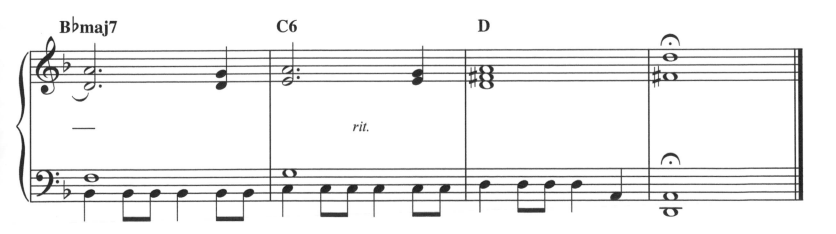

IN THE MIDNIGHT HOUR

Words and Music by STEVE CROPPER
and WILSON PICKETT

Moderately

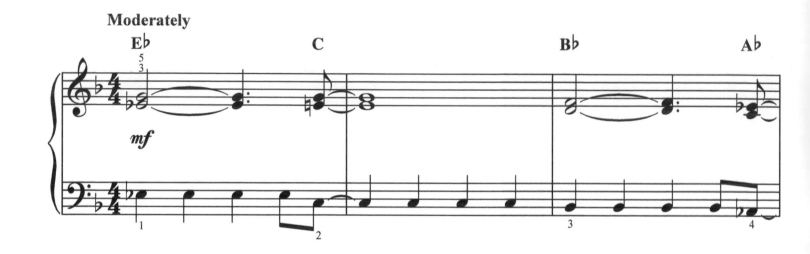

I'm gon - na

(1.,3.) wait   till the mid - night   hour,___
(2.) wait   till the stars   come   out,___

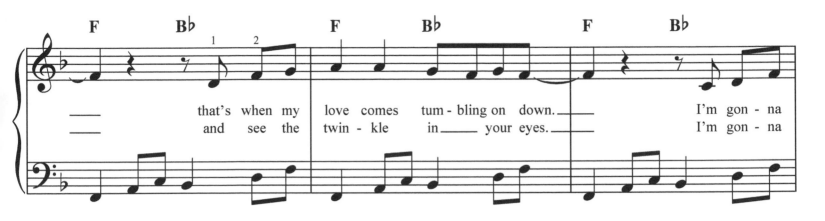

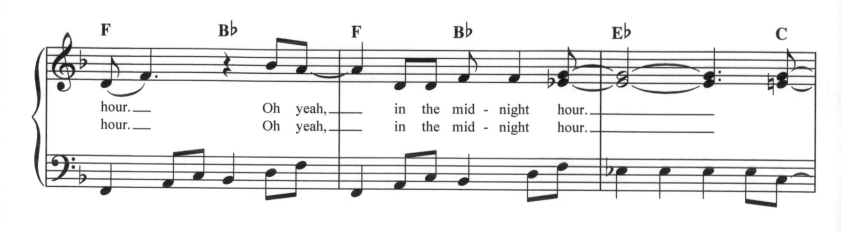

hour.___ Oh yeah,___ in the mid - night hour.___
hour.___ Oh yeah,___ in the mid - night hour.___

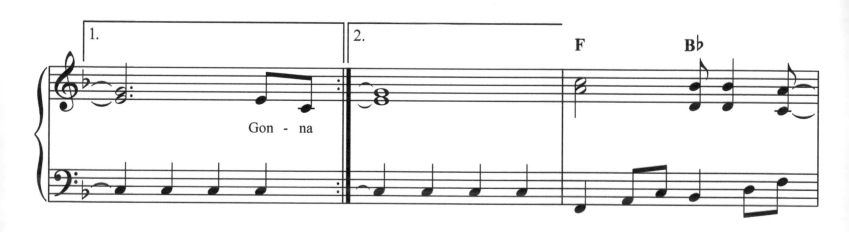

Gon - na

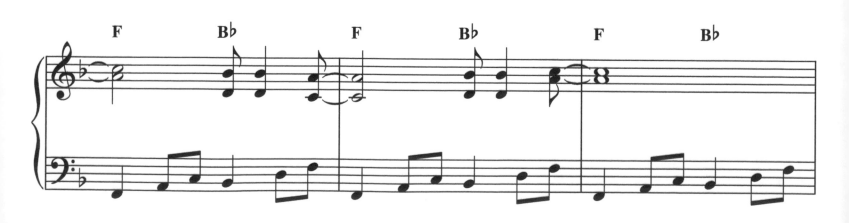

D.S. al Coda

CODA

I'm gon - na

_ you. _

In the mid - night _ hour. _

_ Oh, yeah. _

In the mid - night hour. _

Oh, babe, _

_ you make me feel so

good.

JUST MY IMAGINATION
(Running Away with Me)

Words and Music by NORMAN WHITFIELD
and BARRETT STRONG

70

Don't ev - er let a - noth - er take her love from me or I would sure - ly die. ___

Her love is heav - en - ly, when her arms en - fold me, I hear a ten - der rhap - so-

dy; but in re - al - i - ty, she does - n't e - ven know me.

way with me. No, no, no, no, no, no, no, can't for - get her. ___

LEAN ON ME

Words and Music by
BILL WITHERS

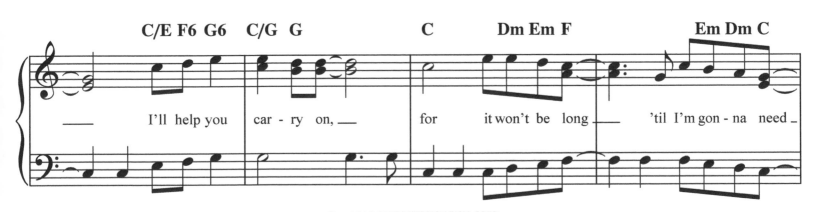

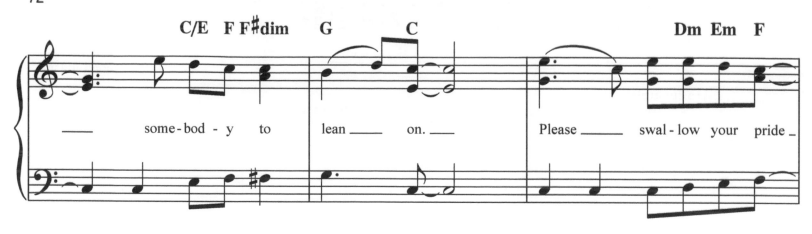

somebody to lean on. Please swallow your pride

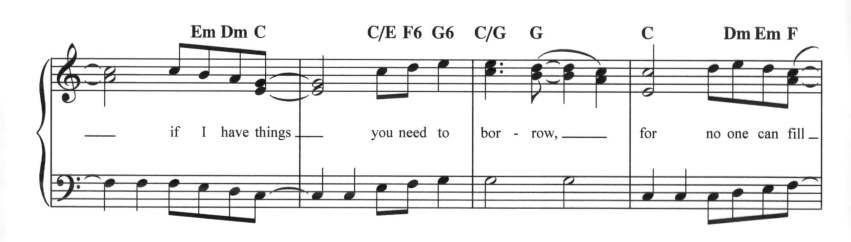

if I have things you need to borrow, for no one can fill

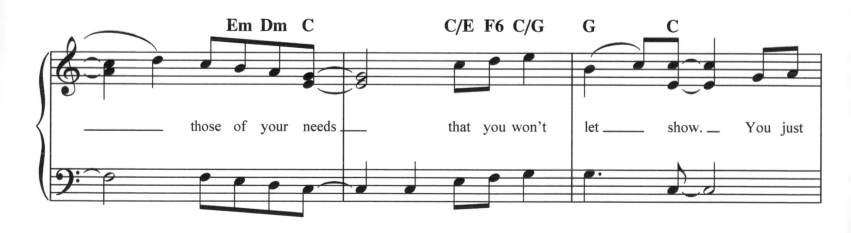

those of your needs that you won't let show. You just

call on me, brother, when you need a hand. We all need somebody to

73

JUST ONCE

Words by CYNTHIA WEIL
Music by BARRY MANN

I did my best, but I guess my best was-n't good e-nough, 'cause
I gave my all, but I think my all may have been too much, 'cause

here we are back where we were be-fore. Seems noth-ing ev-er chang-es, we're
Lord knows, we're not get-ting an-y-where. It seems we're al-ways blow-in' what-

back to be-ing strang-ers, won-d'ring if we ought to stay or head on out the
ev-er we've got go-in', and it seems at times with all we've got, we have-n't got a

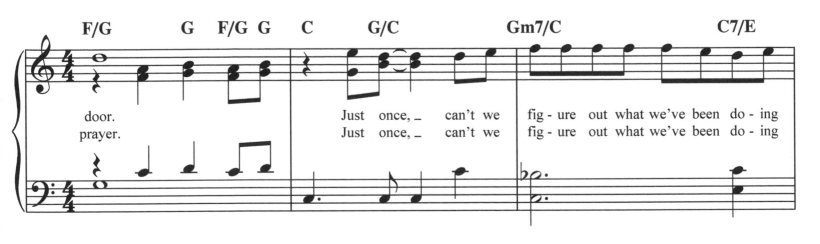

door.
prayer.
Just once, _ can't we fig - ure out what we've been do - ing
Just once, _ can't we fig - ure out what we've been do - ing

wrong?
wrong?
Why we nev - er last for ver - y long? What are we
Why the good times nev - er last for long? Where are we

do - ing wrong?
go - ing wrong?
Just once, _ can't we find a way to fi - n'lly make it
Just once, _ can't we find a way to fi - n'lly make it

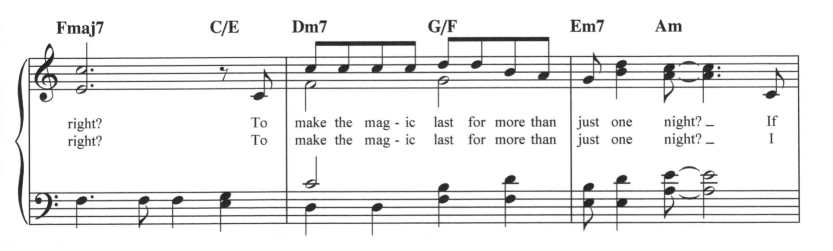

right?
right?
To make the mag - ic last for more than just one night? _ If
To make the mag - ic last for more than just one night? _ I

we could just get to it, I
know we could break through it if

know we could break through it.

we could just get to it just __

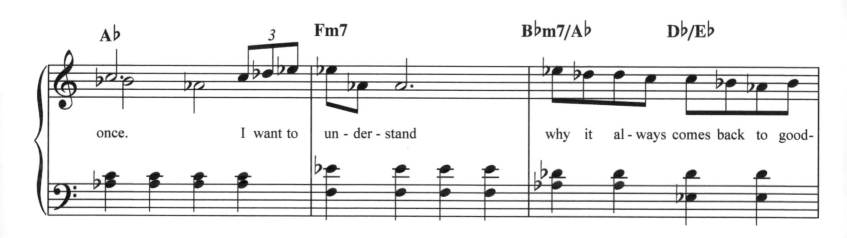

once. I want to un - der - stand

why it al - ways comes back to good-

bye. Why can't we get our - selves in hand

and ad - mit to one an - oth - er we're no good with - out each oth - er? Take the best and make it bet - ter,

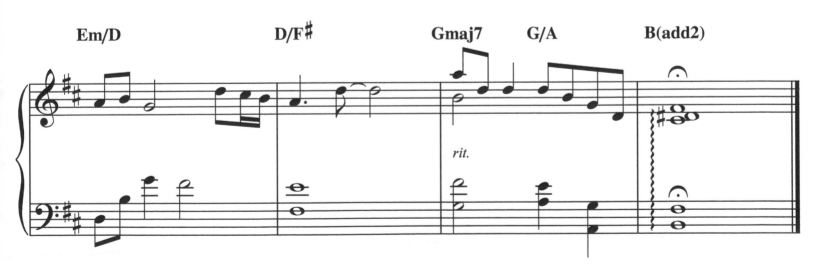

MY GIRL

Words and Music by SMOKEY ROBINSON
and RONALD WHITE

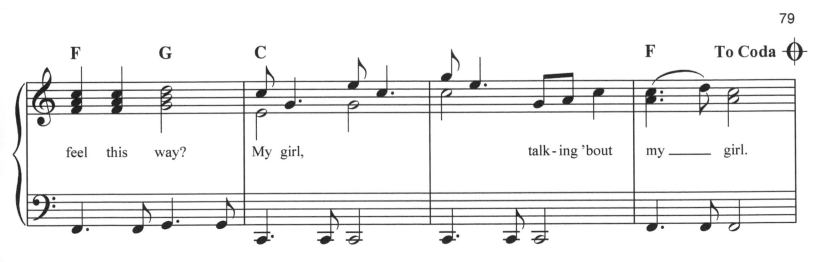

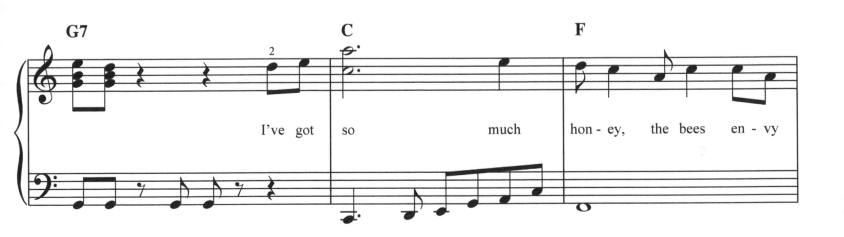

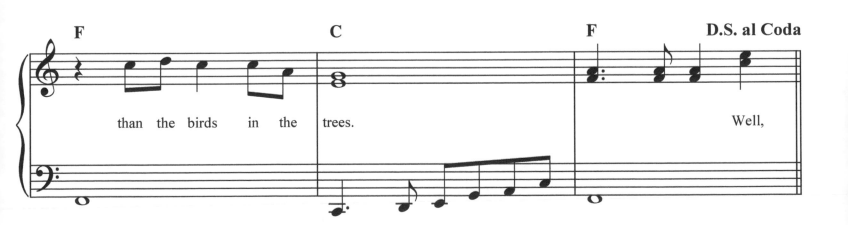

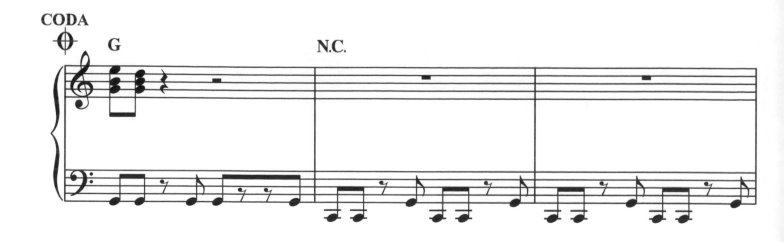

I don't need no mon - ey,

fortune or fame. I've got all the rich-es, ba - by,

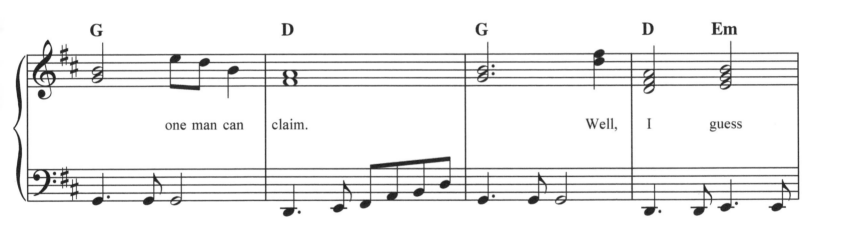

one man can claim. Well, I guess

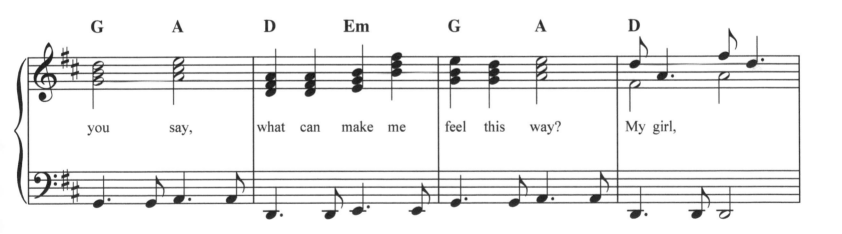

you say, what can make me feel this way? My girl,

talk-ing 'bout my _____ girl.

I've got sun-shine on a cloud-y day with my girl._____ I've

e-ven got the month of May with my girl._____ Talk-ing 'bout,__

talk-ing 'bout,__ talk-ing 'bout__ my girl._____ Woo, my girl._____

_____ That's all I can talk a-bout is my girl._____

LET'S GET IT ON

Words and Music by MARVIN GAYE
and ED TOWNSEND

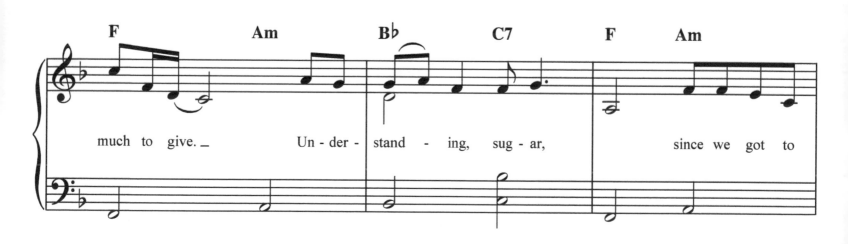

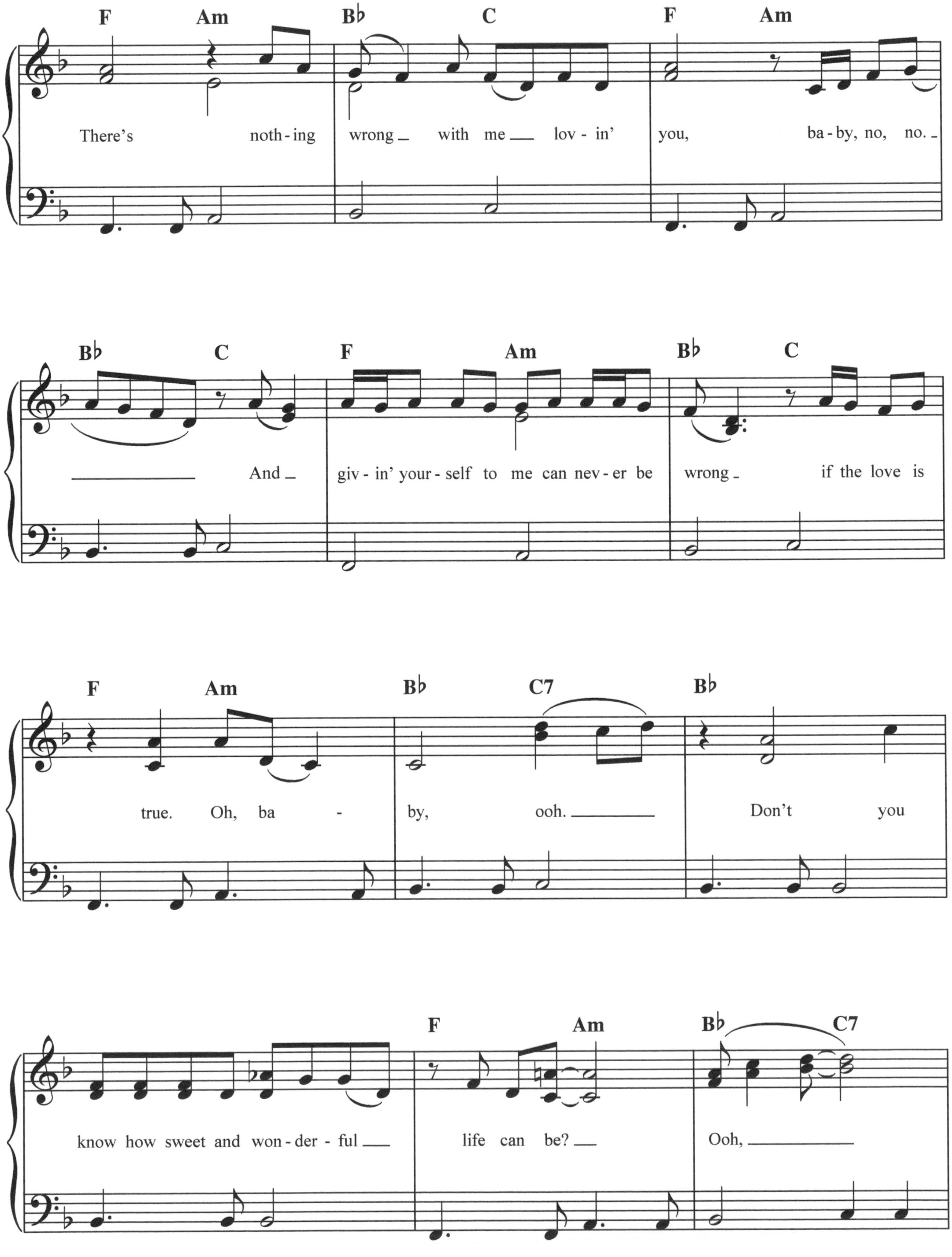
F Am Bb C F Am
There's noth-ing wrong with me lov-in' you, ba-by, no, no.
Bb C F Am Bb C
And giv-in' your-self to me can nev-er be wrong if the love is
F Am Bb C7 Bb
true. Oh, ba - by, ooh. Don't you
F Am Bb C7
know how sweet and won-der-ful life can be? Ooh,

I'm ask-in' you, ba-by, to get it on with me. Ooh, __ ooh, __

__ ooh. __ I ain't goin' to wor-ry. I ain't goin' to

push. I won't push you, ba-by. _____ Just come on, come on, come on, come on, come on,

ba-by, __ stop beat-in' 'round the bush. Hey, __ let's get it

If the spir-it moves you, let me groove you. Good, let your love come down, oh.

Get it on, _____ come on, ba - by. _____ Do you know I

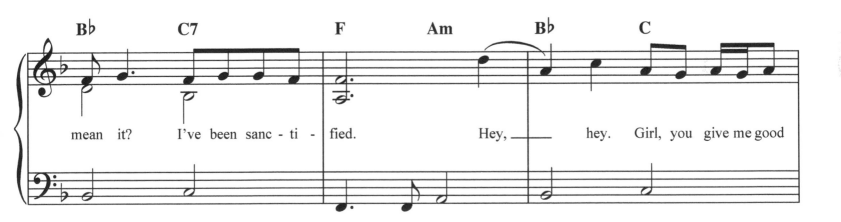

mean it? I've been sanc-ti-fied. Hey, _____ hey. Girl, you give me good

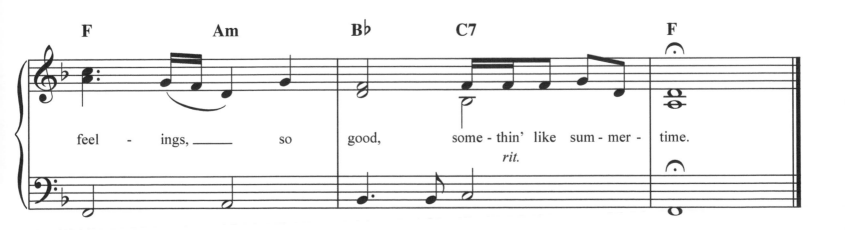

feel - ings, _____ so good, some-thin' like sum-mer - time.

LET'S STAY TOGETHER

Words and Music by AL GREEN,
WILLIE MITCHELL and AL JACKSON, JR.

Am7 ... **Gm7**

geth - er,_____ lov - ing you wheth - er,

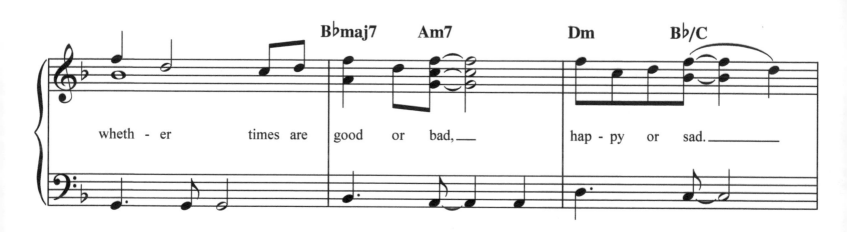

Bbmaj7 **Am7** **Dm** **Bb/C**

wheth - er times are good or bad,___ hap - py or sad.___

Gm9 **Abmaj7**

Gm7 **Abmaj7** **Gm7**

Wheth - er times are

LOVE TRAIN

Words and Music by KENNETH GAMBLE
and LEON HUFF

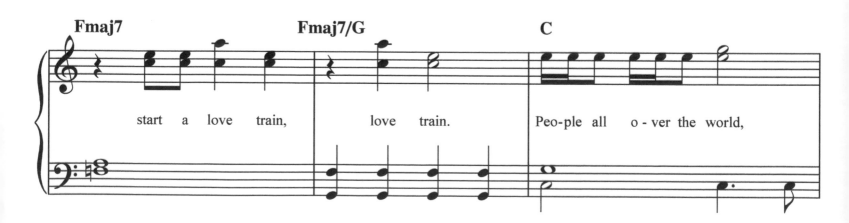

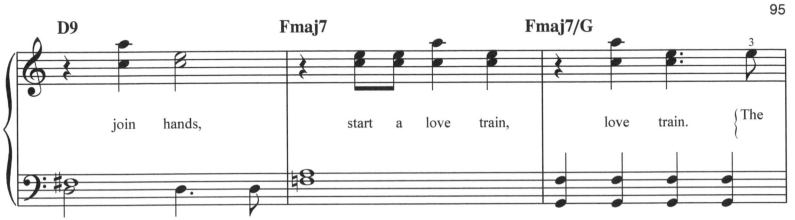

D9   **Fmaj7**   **Fmaj7/G**

join hands,   start a love train,   love train. { The

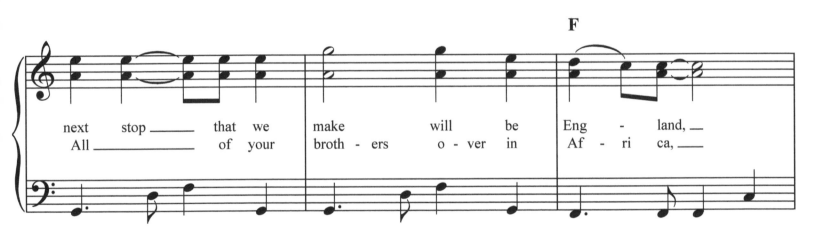

F

next stop ____ that we   make will be   Eng - land, __
All ____ of your   broth - ers o - ver in   Af - ri - ca, __

Fmaj7/G

tell all the folks in   Rus - sia, in Chi - na,
tell all the folks in   E - gypt and Is - rael,

F   **Fmaj7/G**

3   3

too. ____   Don't you know that it's
too. ____   Please don't miss __ this

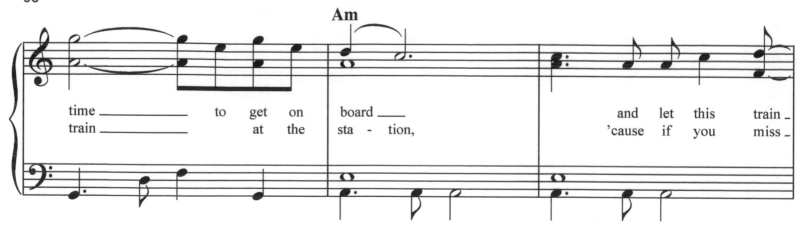

Am

time _____ to get on board _____ and let this train _____
train _____ at the sta - tion, 'cause if you miss _____

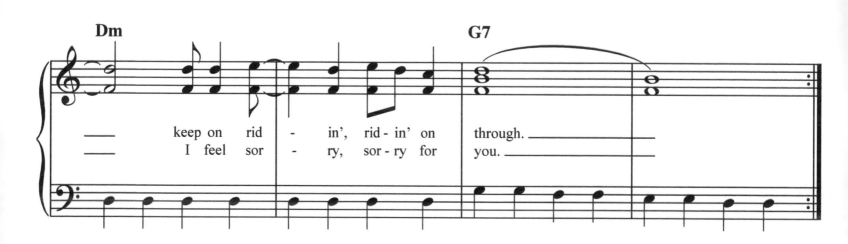

Dm   **G7**

_____ keep on rid - in', rid - in' on through. _____
_____ I feel sor - ry, sor - ry for you. _____

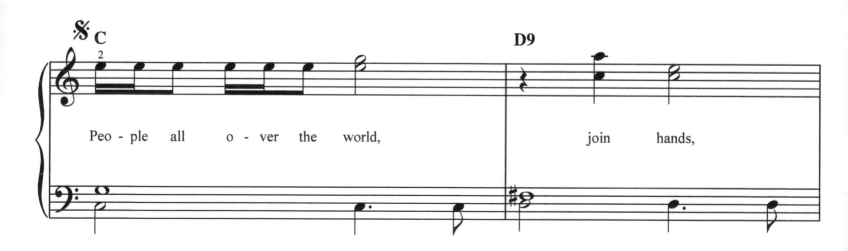

C   **D9**

Peo - ple all o - ver the world, join hands,

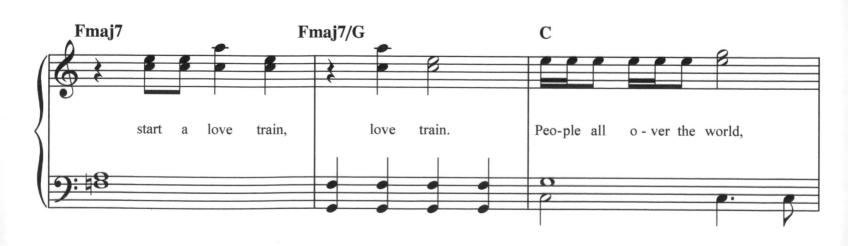

Fmaj7   **Fmaj7/G**   **C**

start a love train, love train. Peo - ple all o - ver the world,

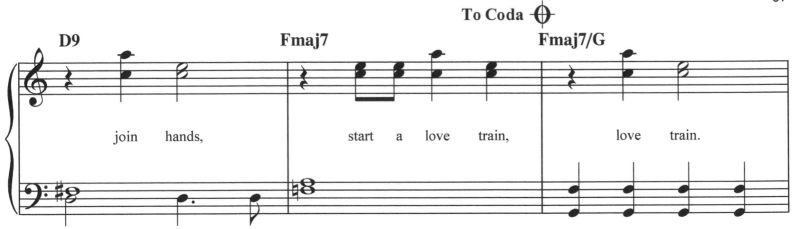

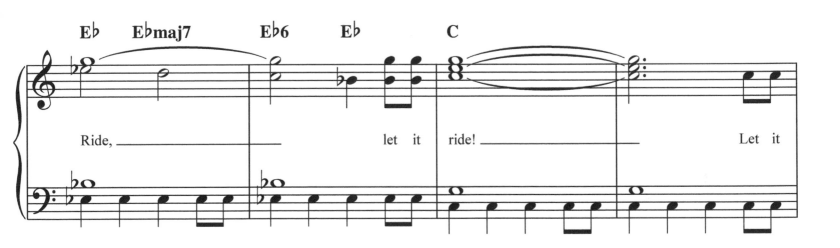

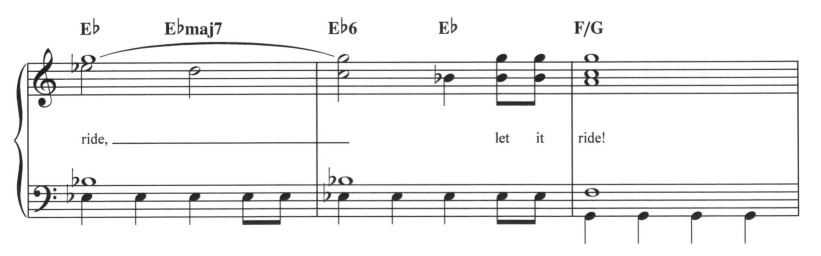

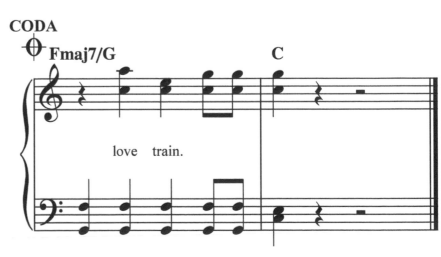

MIDNIGHT TRAIN TO GEORGIA

Words and Music by
JIM WEATHERLY

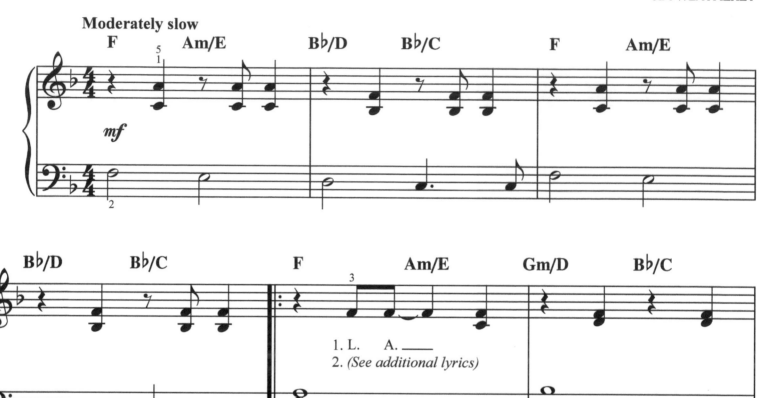

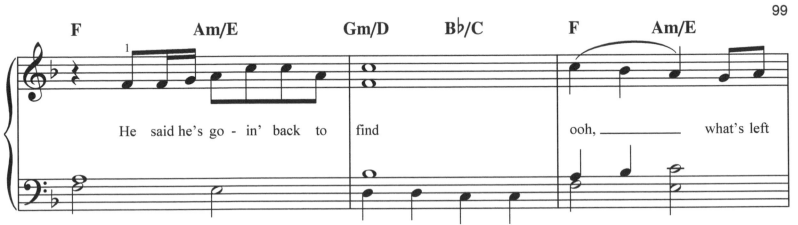

He said he's go - in' back to find ooh, _____ what's left

of his world, _ the world he left be - hind _ not so long,

long a - go. _____ He's leav - in' _____

on that mid - night train to Geor - gia, and he's

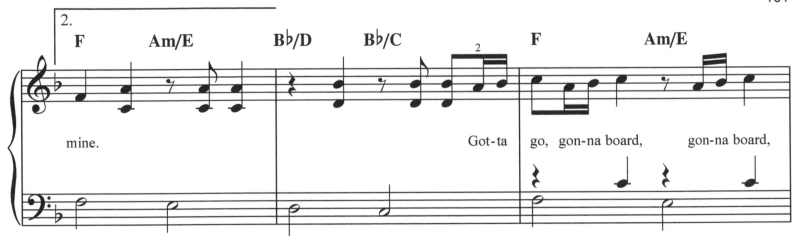

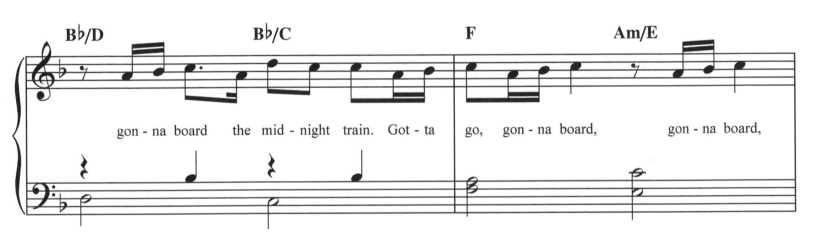

Additional Lyrics

He kept dream-in' that some day he'd be a star,
But he sure found out the hard way that dreams don't always come true.
So he pawned all his hopes and he even sold his old car;
Bought a one-way ticket to the life he once knew.
Oh, yes, he did! He said he would be leavin'....

NEVER CAN SAY GOODBYE

Words and Music by
CLIFTON DAVIS

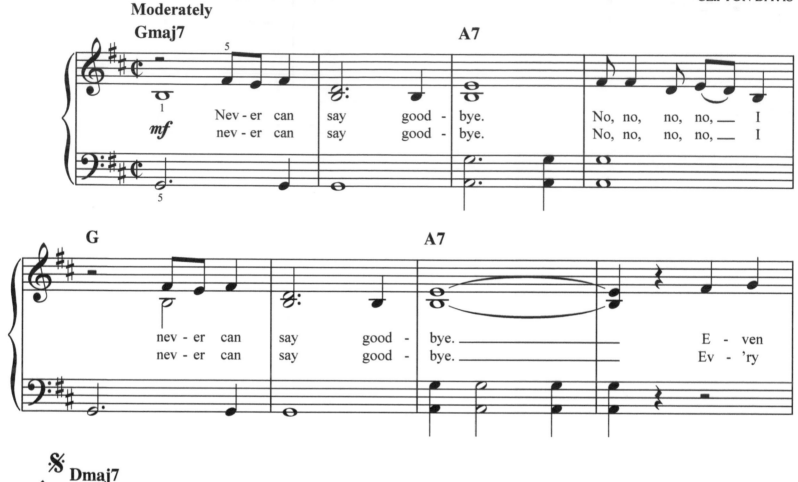

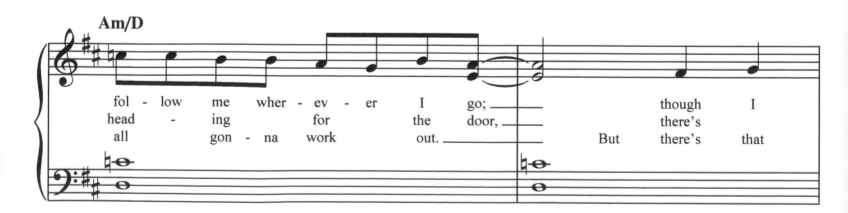

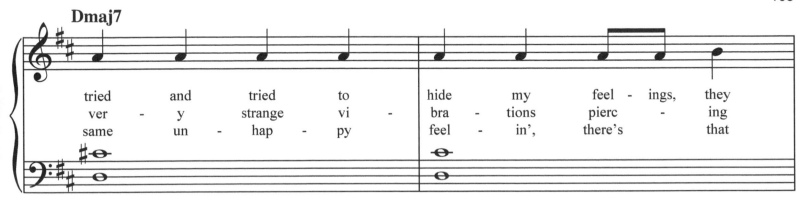

Dmaj7

tried and tried to hide my feel - ings, they
ver - y strange vi - bra - tions pierc - ing
same un - hap - py feel - in', there's that

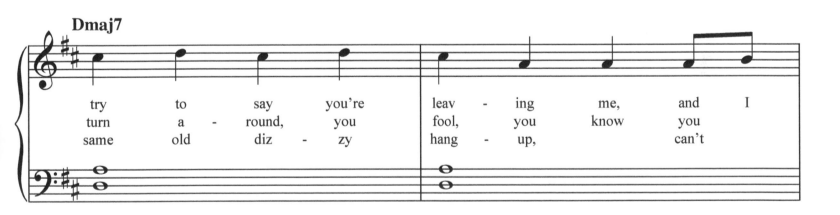

Am/D

al - ways seem to show. Then you
me right to the core. It says
an - guish, there's that doubt. It's that

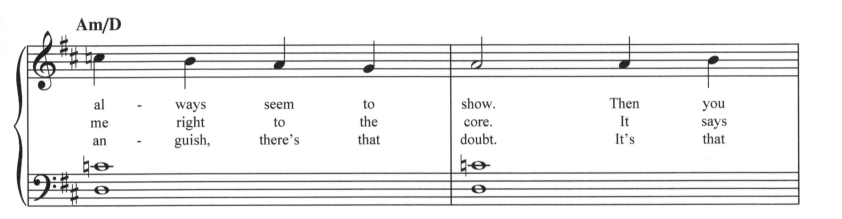

Dmaj7

try to say you're leav - ing me, and I
turn a - round, you fool, you know you
same old diz - zy hang - up, can't

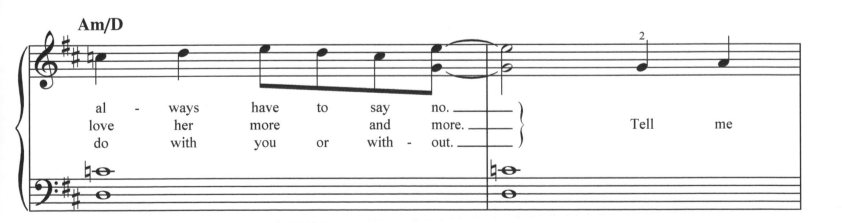

Am/D

al - ways have to say no. Tell me
love her more and more.
do with you or with - out.

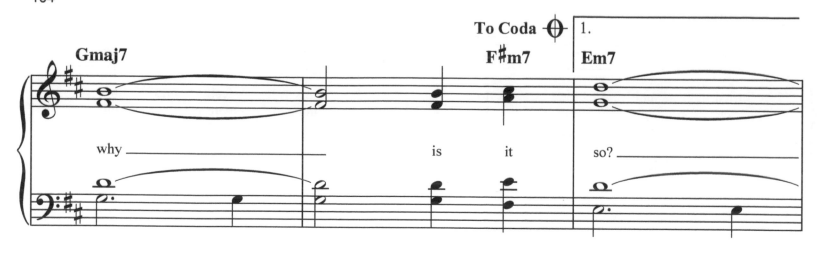

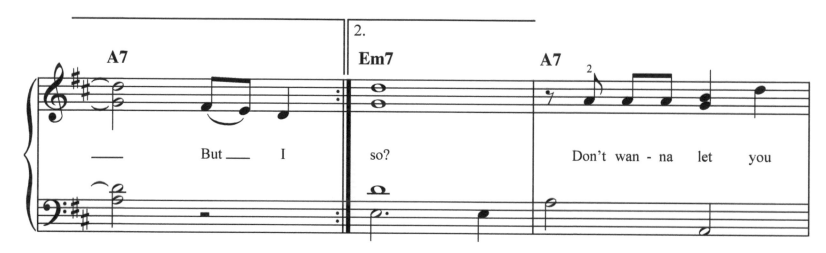

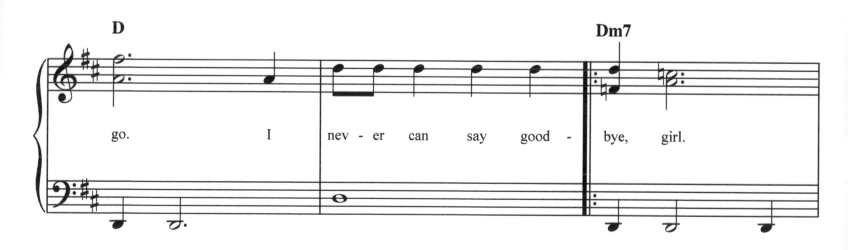

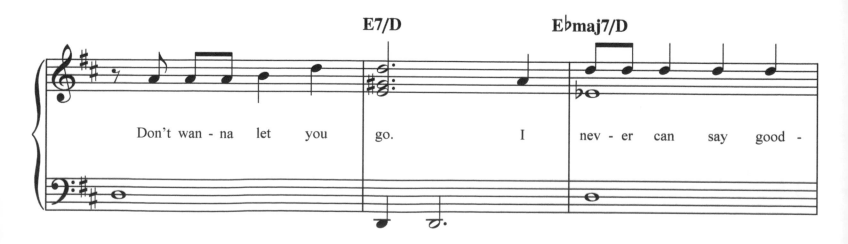

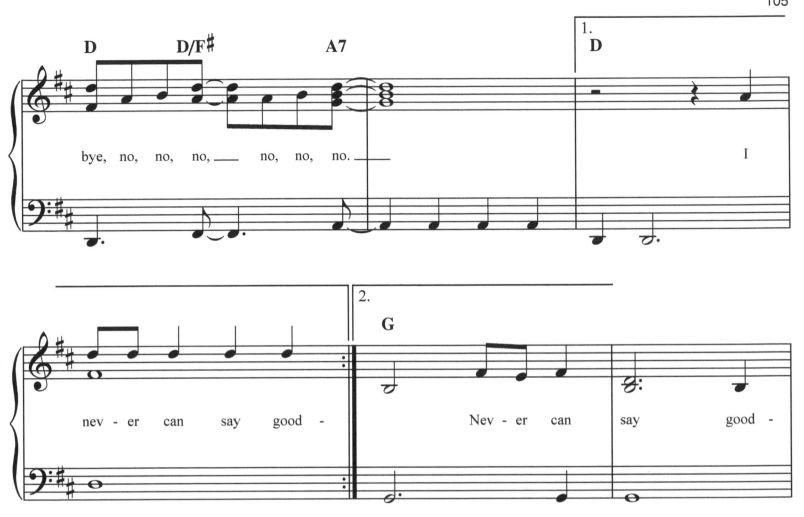

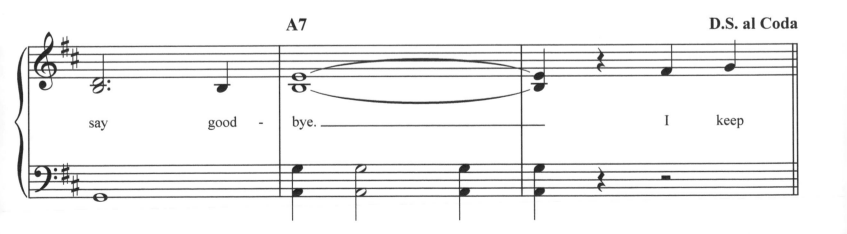

106

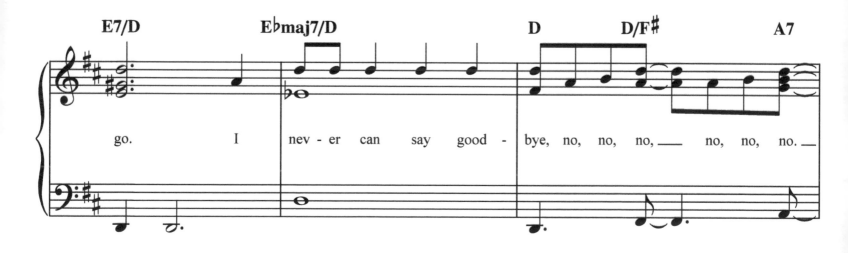

(You Make Me Feel Like)
A NATURAL WOMAN

Words and Music by GERRY GOFFIN,
CAROLE KING and JERRY WEXLER

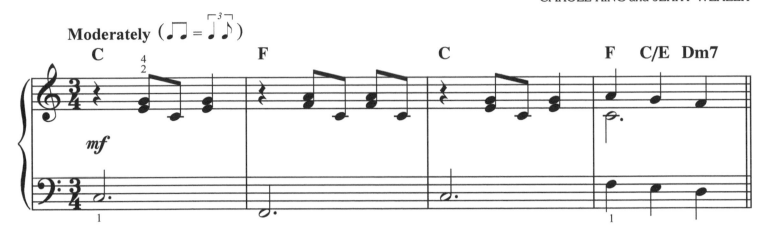

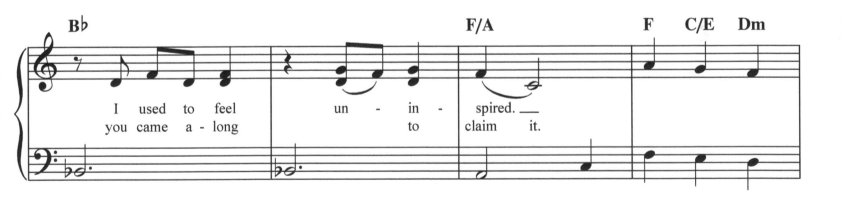

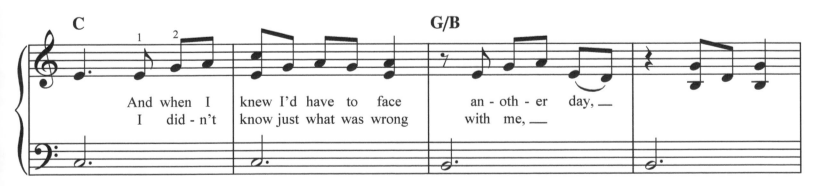

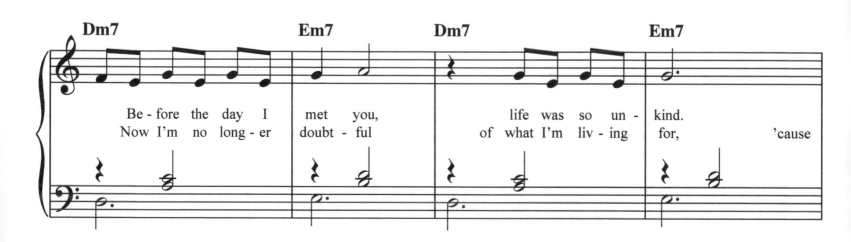

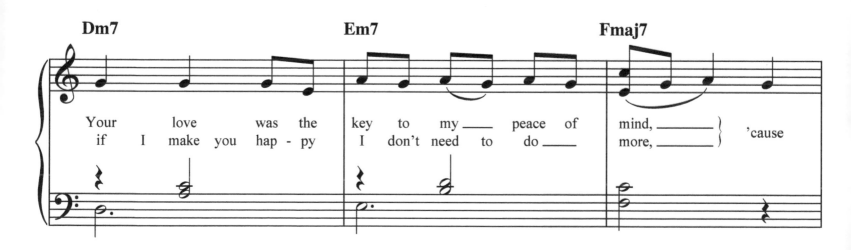

you make me _____ feel like a _____ nat - u - ral

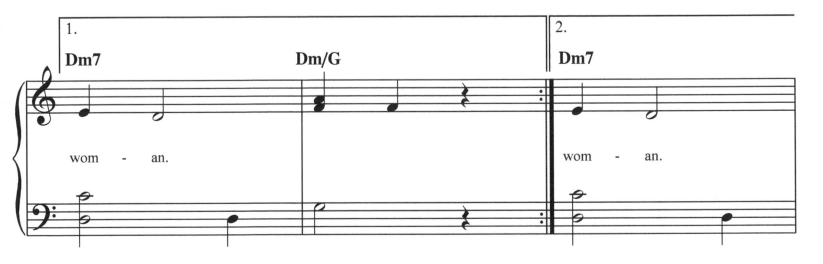

1.
wom - an.

2.
wom - an.

Oh, _____ ba - by, what you've

done to me! _____ (What you've done to me!) _____ You _____ make me

110

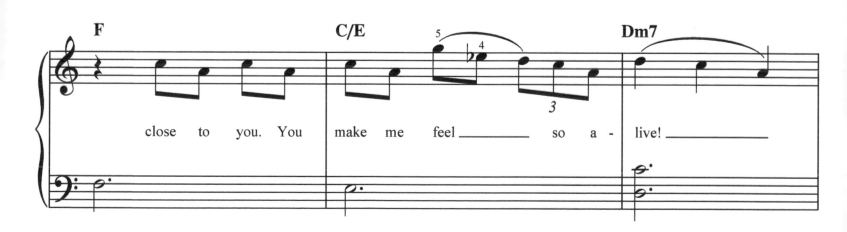

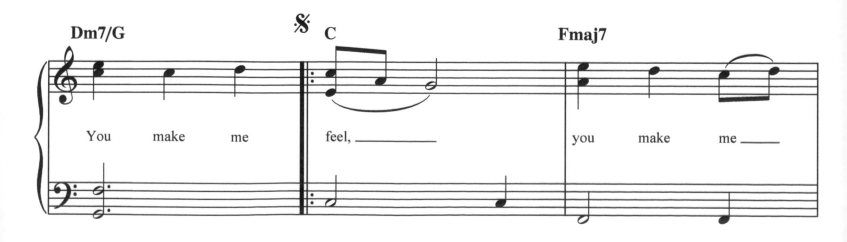

PEOPLE GET READY

Words and Music by
CURTIS MAYFIELD

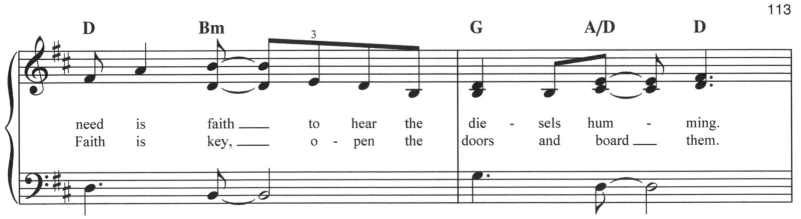

need is faith ____ to hear the die - sels hum - ming.
Faith is key, ____ o - pen the doors and board ____ them.

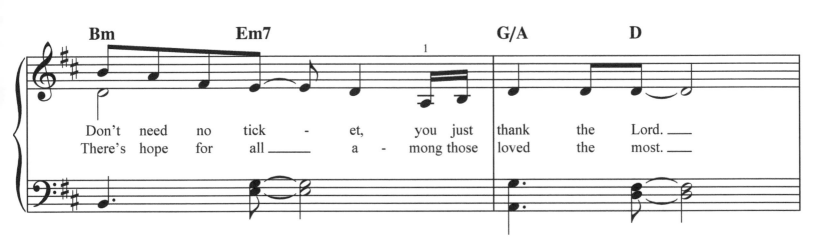

Don't need no tick - et, you just thank the Lord. ____
There's hope for all ____ a - mong those loved the most. ____

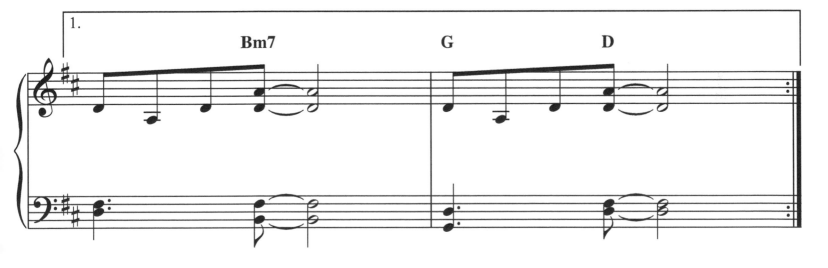

1.

2.

There ain't no room ___ for the hope - less sin - ner ___ who would

hurt all man - kind just to save ___ his own. ___ Have

pit - y on those ___ whose choic - es grow thin - ner ___ so there's

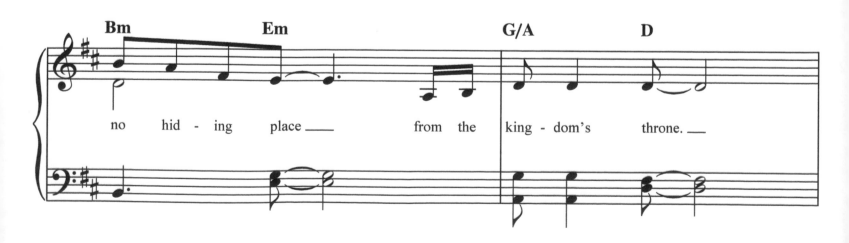

no hid - ing place ___ from the king - dom's throne. ___

PROUD MARY

Words and Music by
JOHN FOGERTY

And I nev - er lost_____ one min - ute of sleep - in',
But I nev - er saw_____ the good side of the cit - y
You don't have to wor - ry 'cause you have no mon - ey.

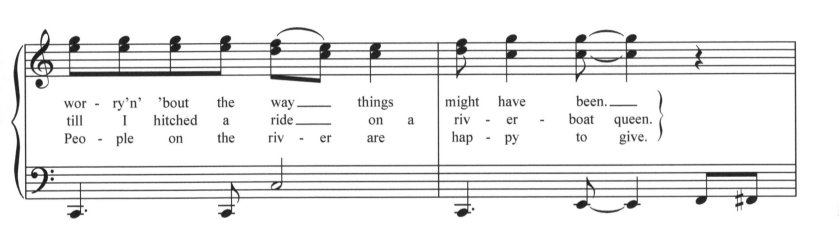

wor - ry'n' 'bout the way_____ things might have been._____
till I hitched a ride_____ on a riv - er - boat queen.
Peo - ple on the riv - er are hap - py to give.

G

Big wheel_____ keep on turn - in',_____ **Am** proud Mar - y keep on

To Coda

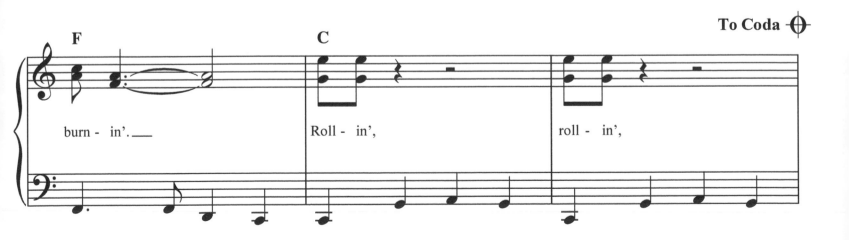

F burn - in'._____ **C** Roll - in', roll - in',

1.

roll - in' on the riv - er.

2.

roll - in' on the riv - er.

Bb   G   Bb   G

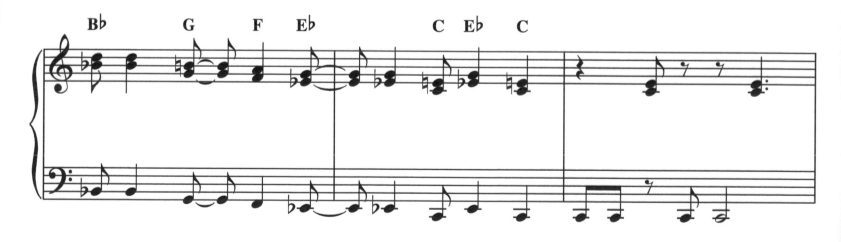

Bb   G   F   Eb   C   Eb   C

D.S. al Coda

CODA

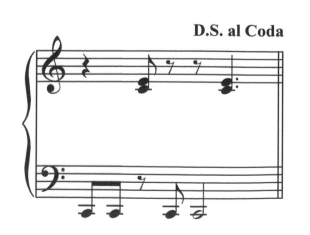

roll - in' on the riv - er.

A RAINY NIGHT IN GEORGIA

Words and Music by
TONY JOE WHITE

1. Hov - erin' by my suit-case, tryin' to find a warm place to
2., 3. *(See additional lyrics)*

spend the night; a heav - y rain a - fall - in';

seems I hear your voice __ call - in', "It's all right."

A rain-y night in Geor-gia, a rain-y night in

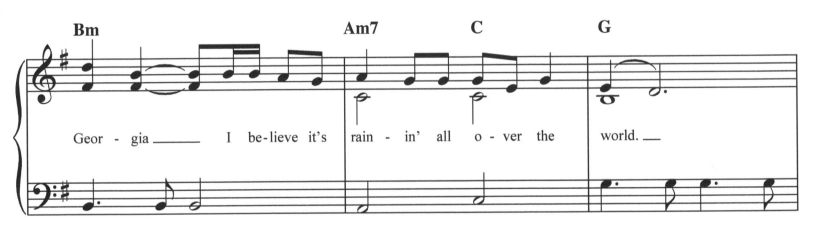

Geor - gia _____ I be-lieve it's rain - in' all o - ver the world. __

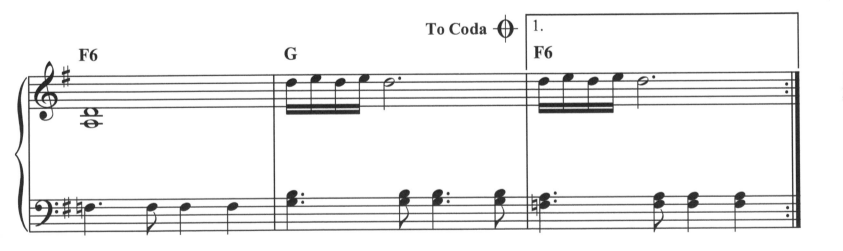

To Coda ⊕ |1.

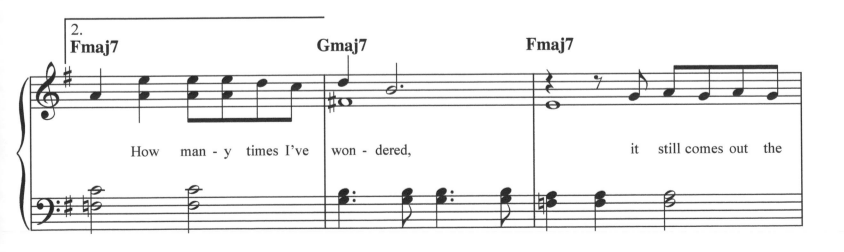

2.

How man-y times I've won-dered, it still comes out the

same;   no mat - ter how you look at it, think of it,   you

just got to   do ___ your own   thing. ___

D.S. al Coda

rit.

Additional Lyrics

2. Neon signs a-flashin'
   Taxi cabs and busses passin' through the night;
   The distant moanin' of a train
   Seems to play a sad refrain to the night:
   Chorus

3. I find me a place in a boxcar,
   So I take out my guitar to pass some time;
   Late at night when it's hard to rest,
   I hold your picture to my chest, and I'm all right.
   Chorus

RESPECT YOURSELF

Words and Music by MACK RICE
and LUTHER INGRAM

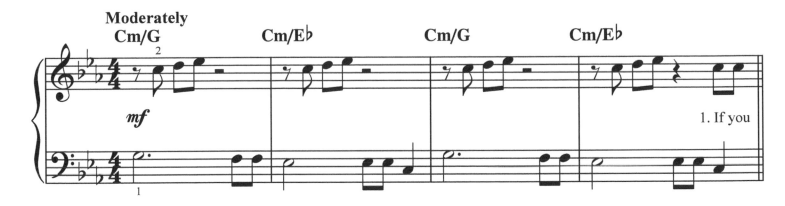

get out the way and let the gen - tle - man do his thing. _____

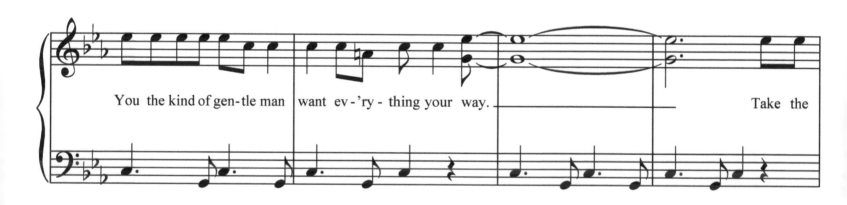

You the kind of gen-tle man want ev-'ry - thing your way. _____ Take the

Chorus

sheet off your face, boy, it's a brand new day. _____ Re - spect your - self, _

_____ re - spect your - self. _____ 'Cause if you

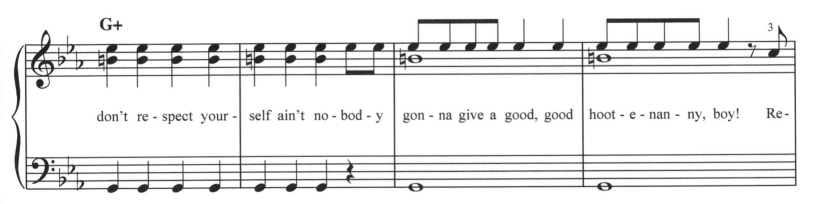

G+

don't re - spect your - self ain't no - bod - y gon - na give a good, good hoot - e - nan - ny, boy! Re -

Cm

1.

spect your - self, _____ re - spect your - self. _____ If you're

2.

spect your - self. _____ Re - spect your - self. ___

Additional Lyrics

2. If you're walking around thinking that the world
Owes you something 'cause you're here,
You're going out the world backward like you did
When you first came 'ere.
Keep talking about the president won't stop air pollution.
Put your hand over your mouth when you cough; that'll help the solution.
You cuss around women folk, don't even know their name,
Then you're dumb enough to think it makes you a big ole man.
Chorus

RESPECT

Words and Music by
OTIS REDDING

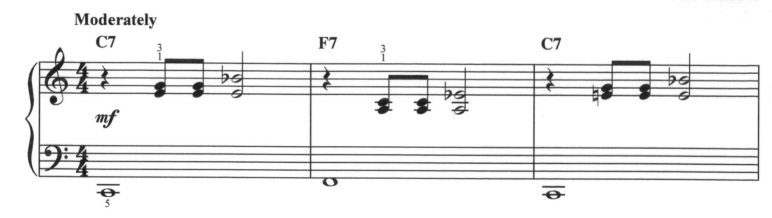

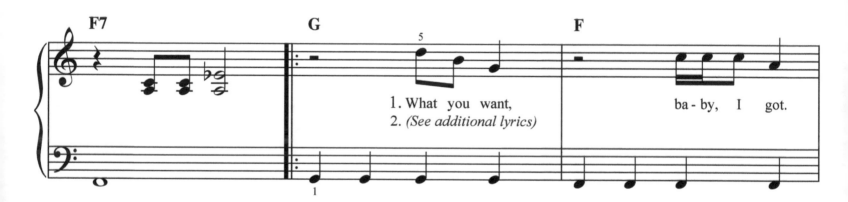

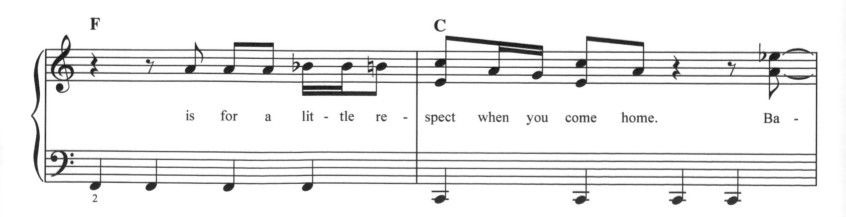

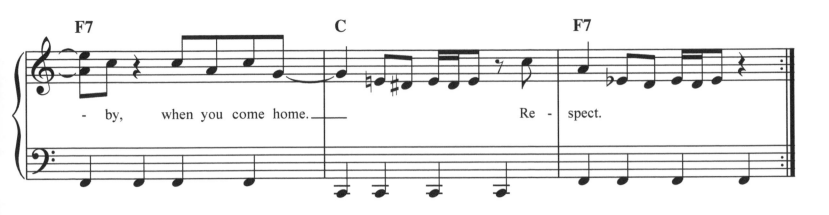

- by, when you come home.___ Re - spect.

3. I'm out__ to give you all my mon - ey but all I'm ask - in'
4. *(See additional lyrics)*

in re - turn, hon - ey, is to give me my prop - er re - spect when you get

home. Yeah, ba - by, when you get home.

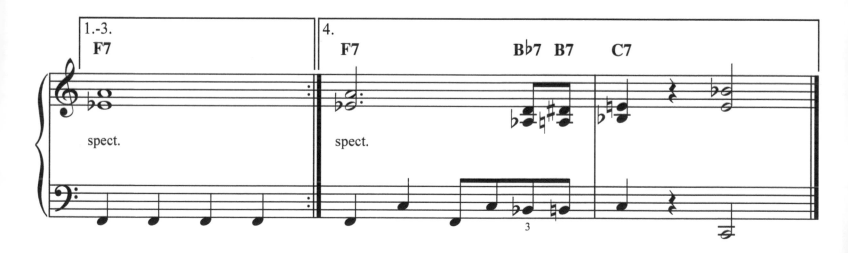

Additional Lyrics

2. I ain't gonna do you wrong while you gone.
   I ain't gonna do you wrong 'cause I don't wanna.
   All I'm askin' is for a little respect, when you come home.
   Baby, when you come home, respect.

4. Ooh, your kisses, sweeter than honey,
   And guess what, so here's my money,
   All I want you to do for me is give it to me when you get home.
   Yeah, baby, when you get home.

RIGHT PLACE, WRONG TIME

Words and Music by
MAC REBENNACK

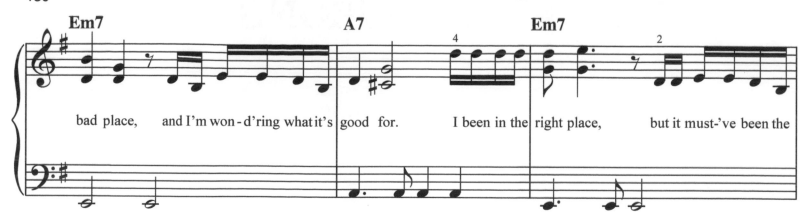

bad place,   and I'm won-d'ring what it's good for.   I been in the right place,   but it must-'ve been the

wrong time.   My head was in a bad place,   but I'm hav-ing such a good time.

I've been run-ning, try'n' to catch, hung up in my mind; —   just got to give my-self a good

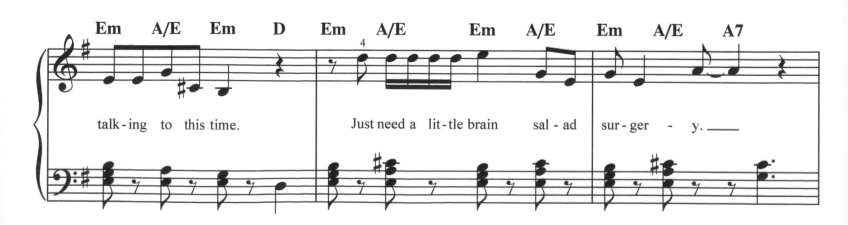

talk-ing to this time.   Just need a lit-tle brain sal - ad sur-ger - y. __

I got to cure my in-se-cur-i-ty. ___ But I been in the wrong place, but it must-'ve been the

right time. I been in the right place, but it must-'ve been the wrong song. I been in the

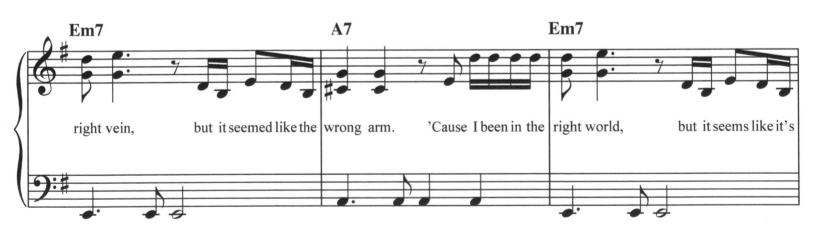

right vein, but it seemed like the wrong arm. 'Cause I been in the right world, but it seems like it's

wrong, wrong, wrong, — wrong, wrong.

Slip- ping, dodg- ing, sneak - ing, creep- ing,

hid-ing out down the street. See my life shak-ing with ev-'ry who I meet.

Re-friend con-fu - sion is mak-ing it-self clear. _ Won-der which way do I go to

get on out - ta here? 'Cause I been in the right place, but it must-'ve been the

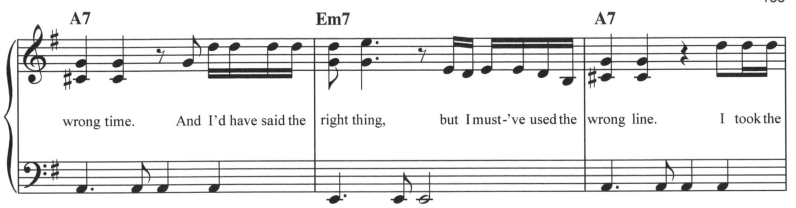

wrong time. And I'd have said the | right thing, | but I must-'ve used the | wrong line. I took the

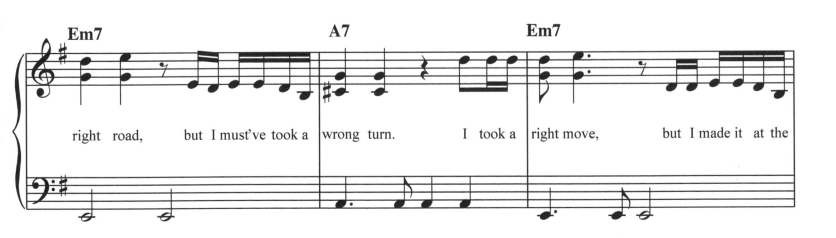

right road, | but I must've took a | wrong turn. I took a | right move, | but I made it at the

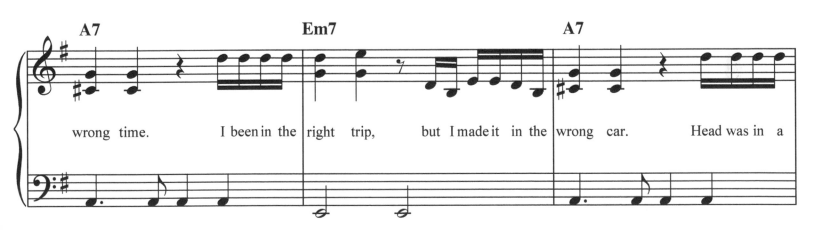

wrong time. I been in the | right trip, | but I made it in the | wrong car. Head was in a

good place, | and I'm won-d'ring what it's | bad for. 'Cause my skull was in a | bad place...

SIGNED, SEALED, DELIVERED I'M YOURS

Words and Music by STEVIE WONDER,
SYREETA WRIGHT, LEE GARRETT
and LULA MAE HARDAWAY

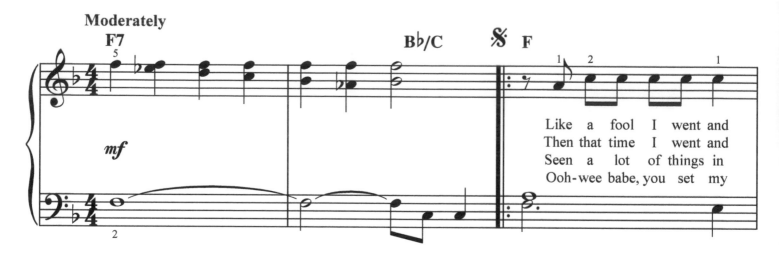

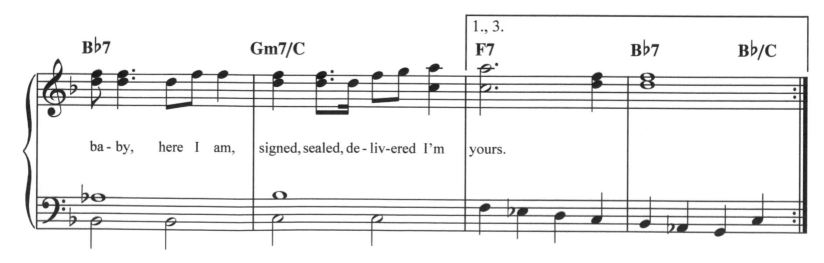

yours. Here I am, ba - by,

signed, sealed, de - liv - ered I'm yours.

Here I am, ba - by, signed, sealed, de - liv - ered I'm

To Coda ⊕

yours. I've done a lot of fool - ish things, that I real - ly did - n't

D.S. al Coda
(with repeat)

mean. Hey, — hey, yeah, yeah, did-n't I, oh ba - by.

CODA

mean. I could be a brok-en man, but here I am with your fu-ture, got your fu-

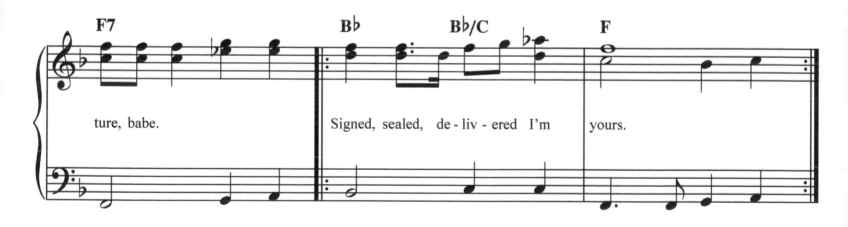

ture, babe. Signed, sealed, de-liv-ered I'm yours.

Signed, sealed, de-liv-ered I'm yours.

ROCK WITH YOU

Words and Music by
ROD TEMPERTON

Moderately fast

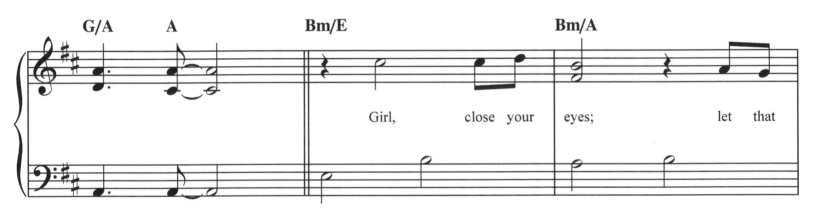

Girl, close your eyes; let that

rhy - thm get in - to you. Don't try to fight

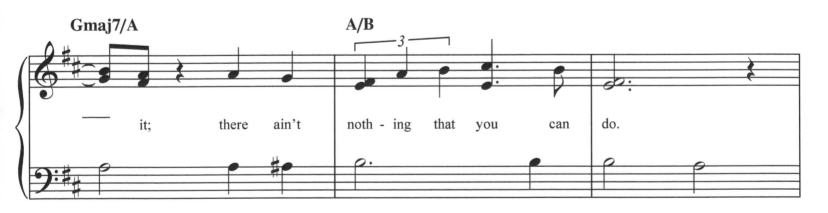

it; there ain't noth - ing that you can do.

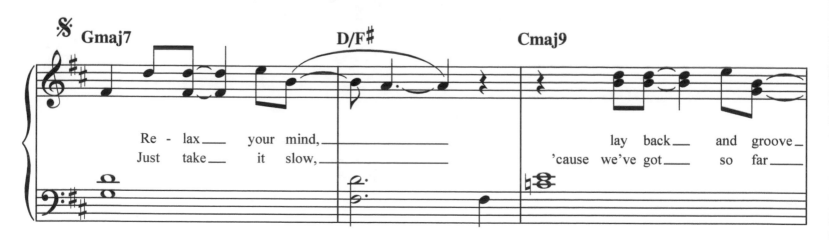

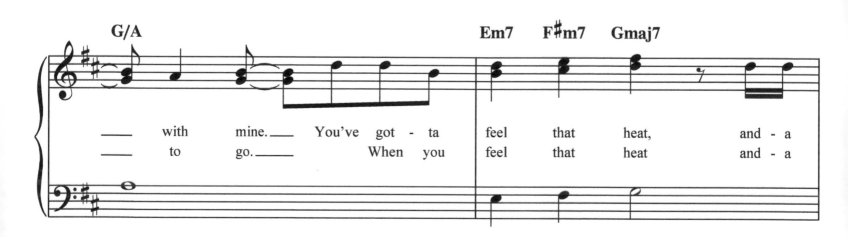

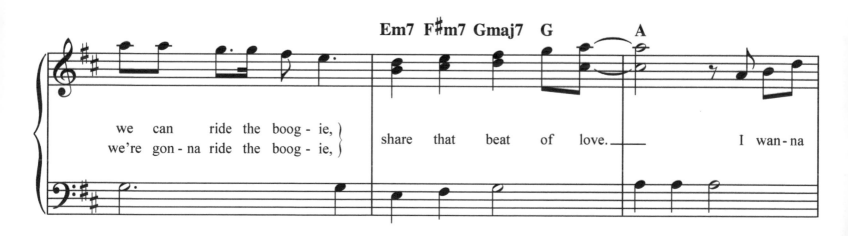

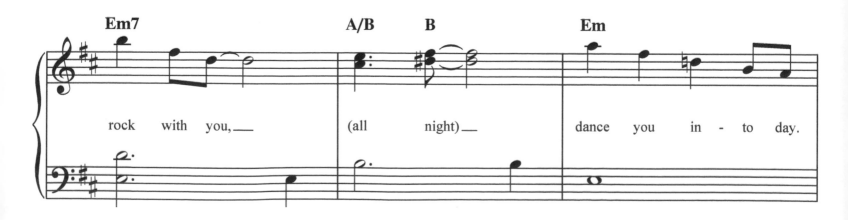

139

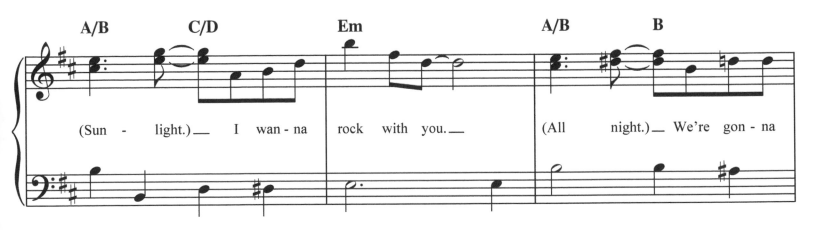

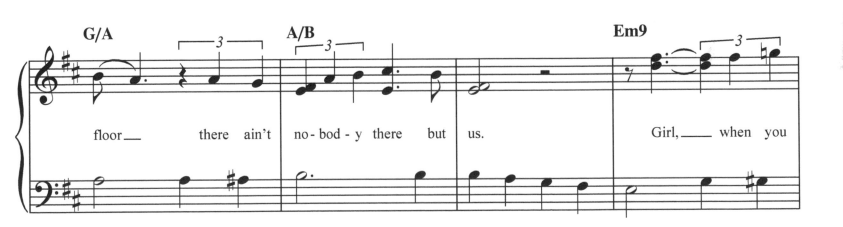

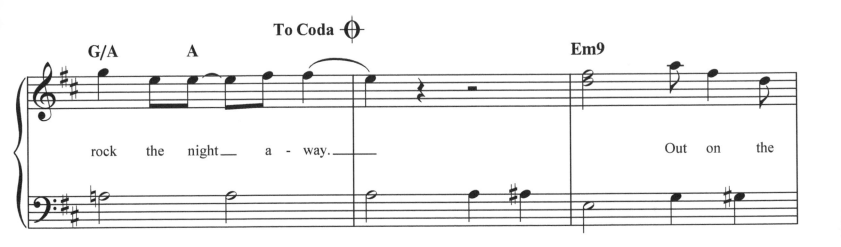

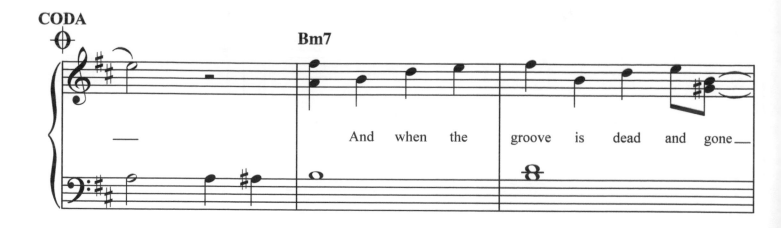

CODA

And when the groove is dead and gone____

you know that love sur - vives_____ so we can

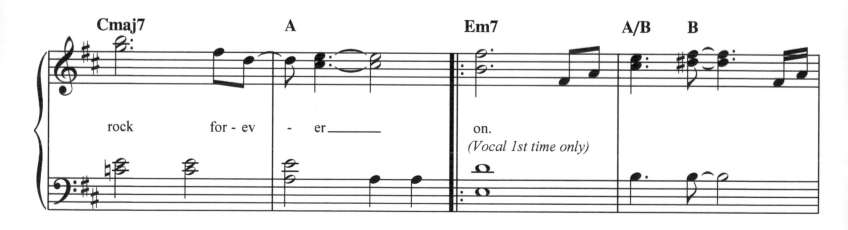

rock for - ev - er_____ on.
(Vocal 1st time only)

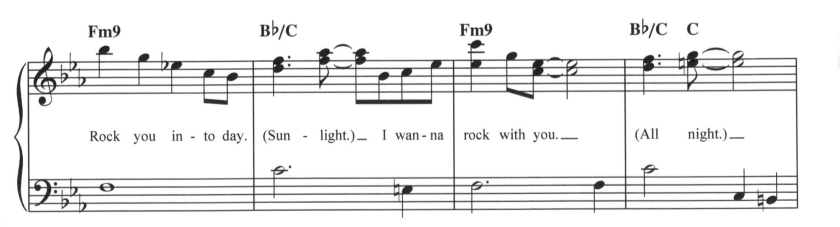

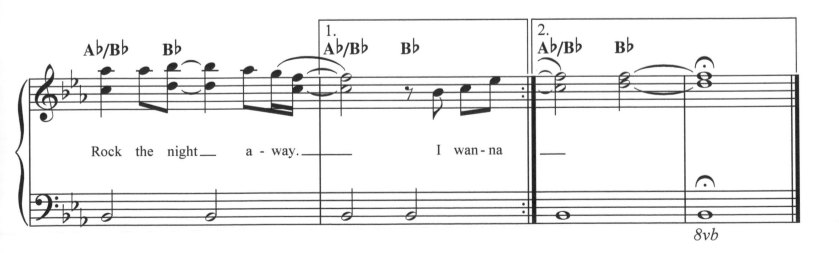

8vb

(Sittin' On)
THE DOCK OF THE BAY

Words and Music by
STEVE CROPPER and OTIS REDDING

roll — a - way. — Oo, I'm just sit - tin' on the dock of the bay, —

wast - in' time. —

To Coda

1.

I

2.

Looks like noth - in's gon - na change; —

ev - 'ry - thing still re - mains the same. —

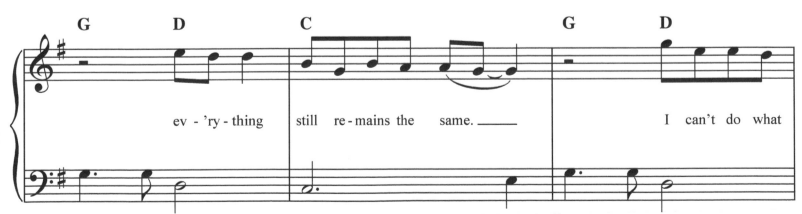

I can't do what

D.S. al Coda

ten peo-ple tell me to do, so I guess I'll re-main _ the same. _

CODA

(whistle)

STAND BY ME

Words and Music by JERRY LEIBER,
MIKE STOLLER and BEN E. KING

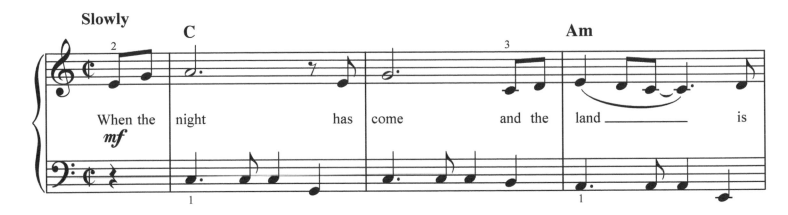

C

me.   Dar - ling,   stand _____ by   me,   won't you

Am   **F**   **G7**   **To Coda**

stand   by   me.   If you're in   need, _   won't you   stand, _   stand by

C

me.   And if the   sky   that we look up -

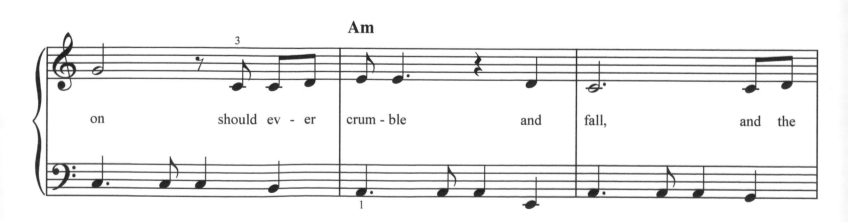

                                                   Am

on   should ev - er   crum - ble   and   fall,   and the

F   **G7**   **C**

moun - tains _____ should fall ___ to the sea, _____

Am

no, I won't _ be a - fraid, _ no, I won't ___ shed a

F   **G7**   **C**

tear just as long _ as you stand, _ stand by me.

D.S. al Coda

Dar - ling, stand _____ by

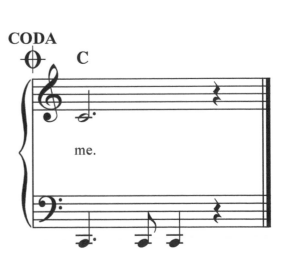

CODA

C

me.

SOUL MAN

Words and Music by ISAAC HAYES
and DAVID PORTER

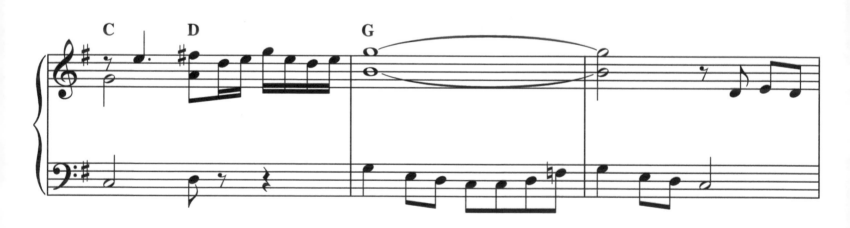

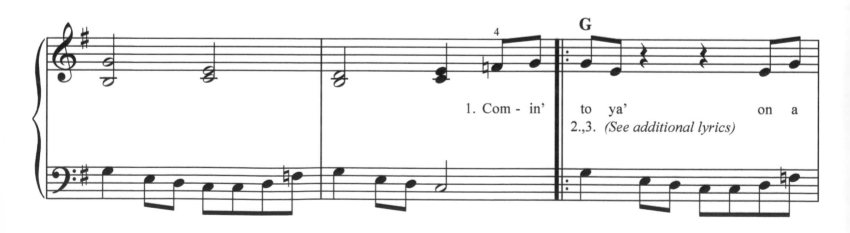

1. Com - in' to ya' on a
2.,3. *(See additional lyrics)*

dust - y road: good__ lov - in', I got a

truck load.__ And when you get it, you got some. So,

Chorus

don't__ wor - ry, 'cause I'm com - in'. I'm a soul man,__

F **G**

I'm a soul man.__ I'm a

F   **G**

soul man, ___   I'm a soul man, ___

1.,2.   **C**   **D**   **3.**   **C**   **D**   **E♭**

2. Got   Grab the rope   and I'll

B♭   **C**   **Dsus**

pull you in,   give you hope,   and   be your on - ly boy - friend

E♭sus   **A♭**

yeah, ___ yeah, ___ yeah, ___ yeah.

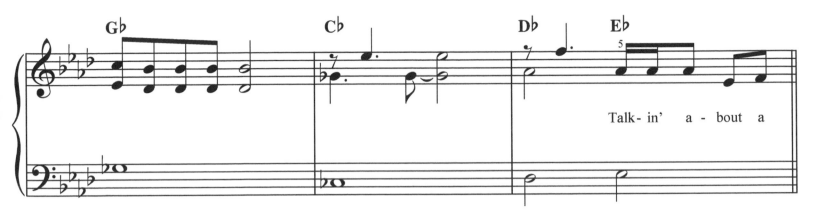

Additional Lyrics

2. Got what I got the hard way,
   And I'll make it better each and every day.
   So, honey, don't you fret,
   'Cause you ain't seen nothin' yet.
   Chorus

3. I was brought up on the south street.
   I learned how to love before I could eat.
   I was educated at Woodstock.
   When I start lovin', oh, I can't stop.
   Chorus

SUPER FREAK

Words and Music by RICK JAMES
and ALONZO MILLER

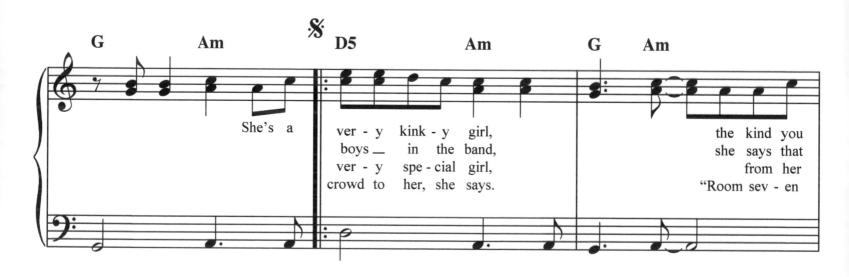

girl's all right _____ with me, yeah. _____

She's a

su - per freak, su - per freak, she's su - per freak - y.

To Coda ⊕

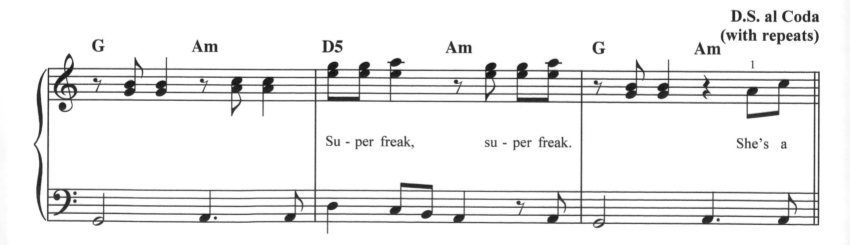

Su - per freak, su - per freak. She's a

D.S. al Coda
(with repeats)

155

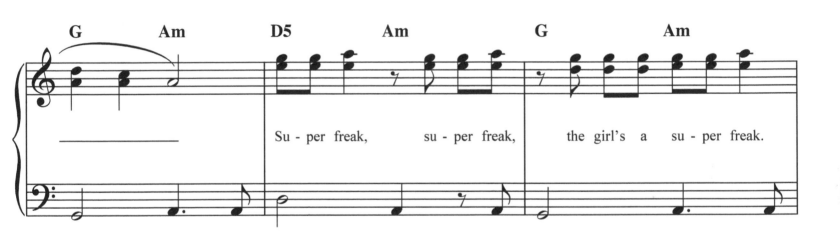

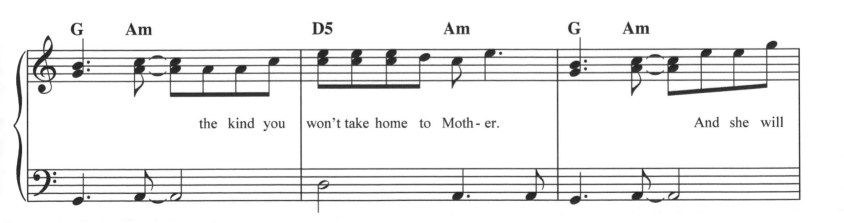

nev - er let your spir - its down, _____ once you get her off the street.

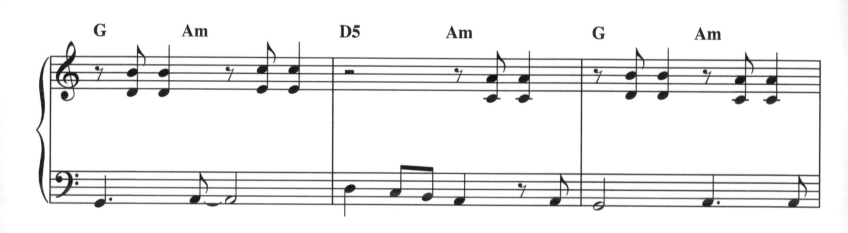

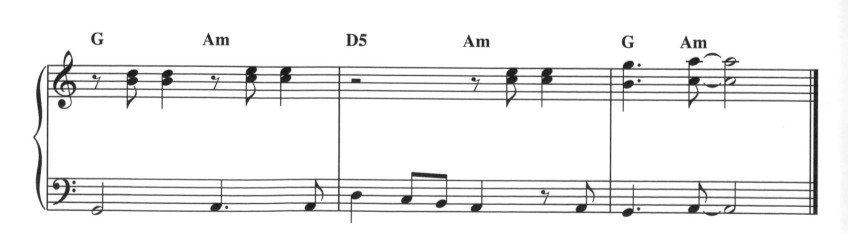

TELL IT LIKE IT IS

Words and Music by GEORGE DAVIS
and LEE DIAMOND

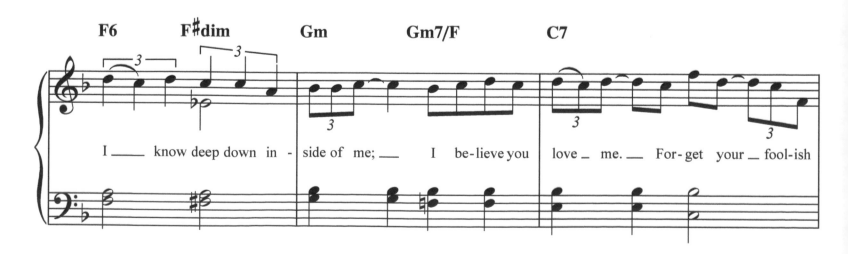

pride. _____

Life is too short ___ to have

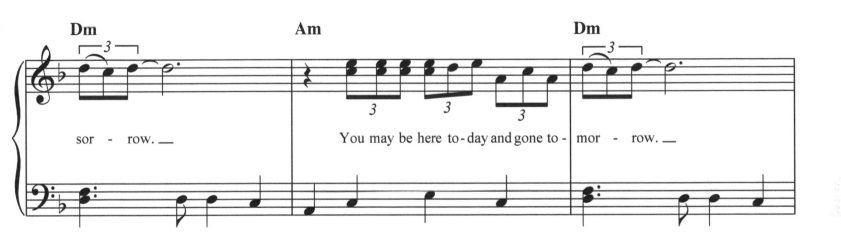

sor - row. __

You may be here to-day and gone to - mor - row. __

You might as well get what you want, so go on and live, ba - by, go on and

live. Tell it like it live. Tell it like it is.

rit.

THESE ARMS OF MINE

Words and Music by
OTIS REDDING

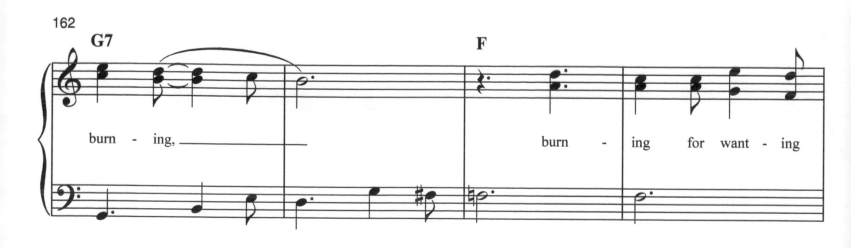

burn - ing, _____ burn - ing for want - ing

you. _____ These arms of mine, _____ they are

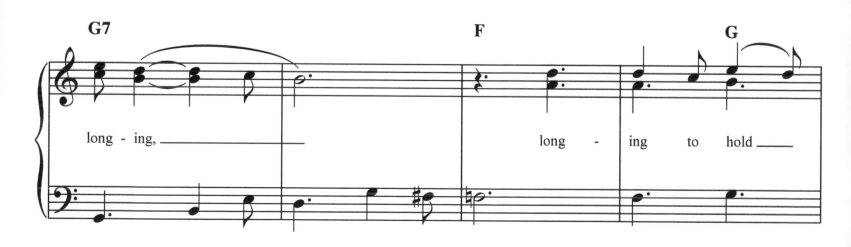

long - ing, _____ long - ing to hold _____

you. _____ And if you _____ would let them

163

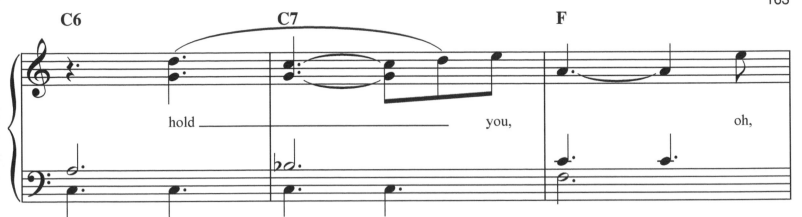

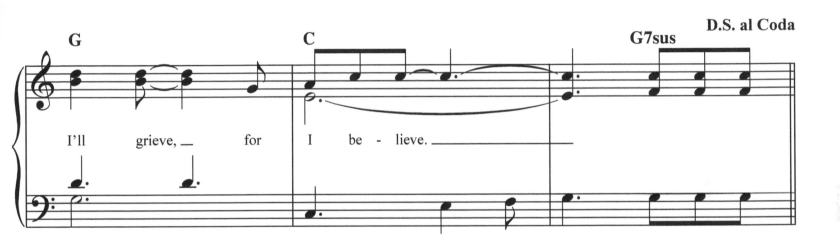

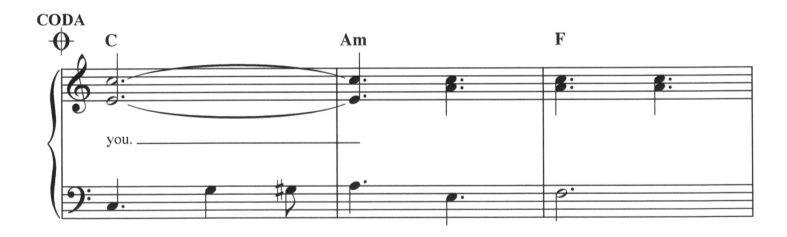

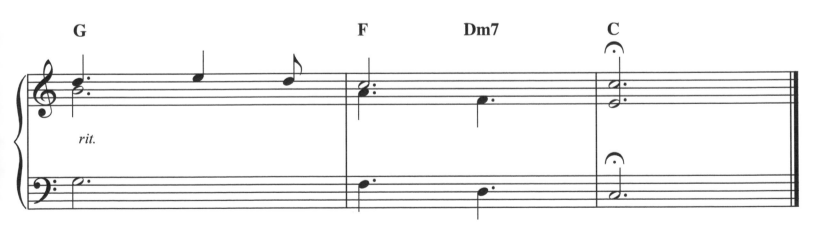

THREE TIMES A LADY

Words and Music by
LIONEL RICHIE

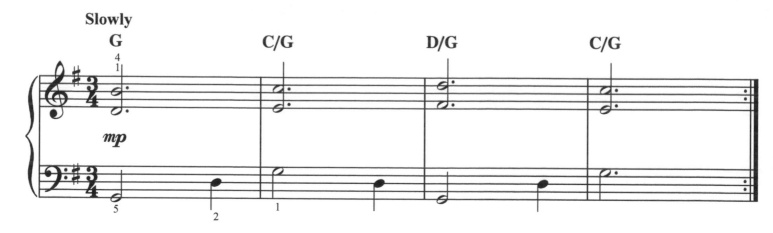

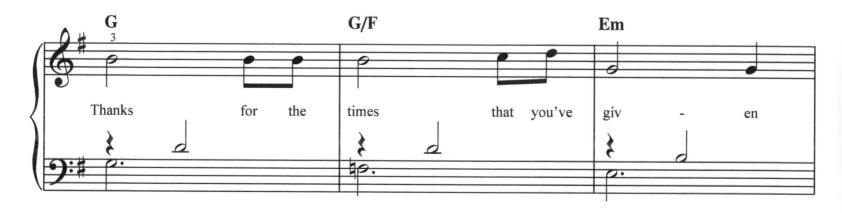

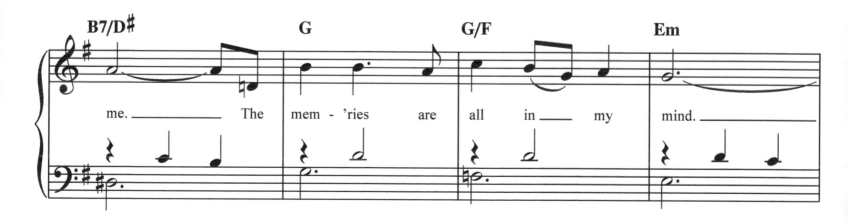

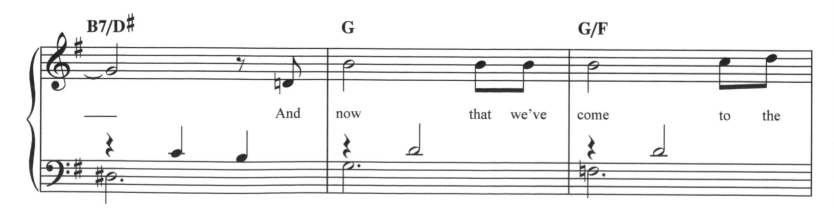

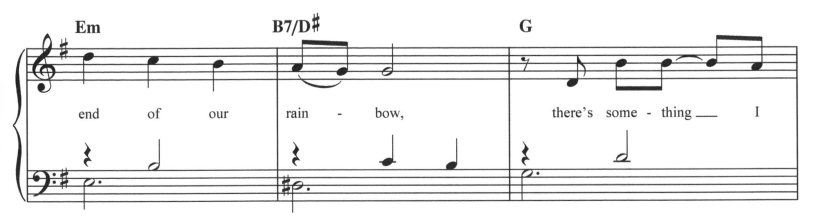

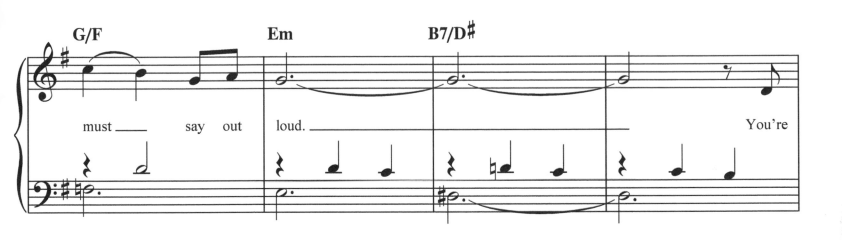

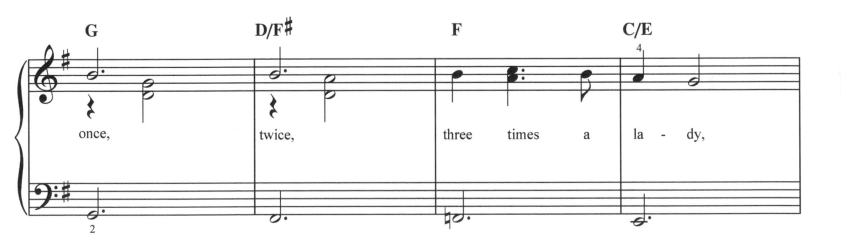

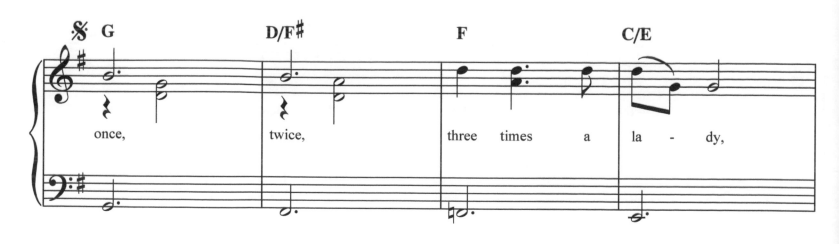

once, twice,

three times a la - dy,

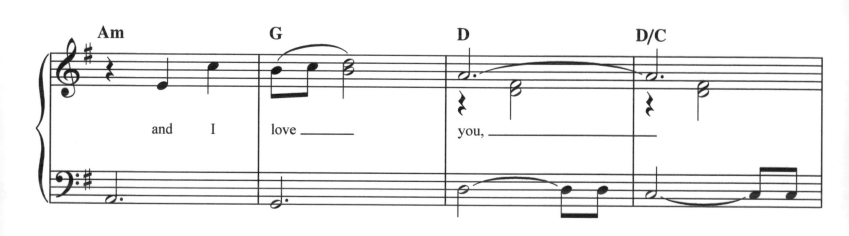

and I love _____ you, _____

I love _____ you.

To Coda ⊕

When we are to - geth - er, the

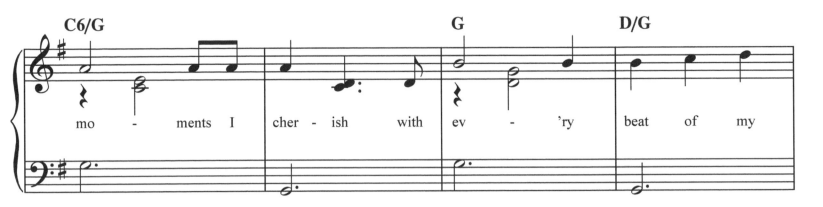

C6/G   G   D/G

mo - ments I cher - ish with ev - 'ry beat of my

C6/G   C6/D   G   D/G

heart. _____ To touch you, to hold you, to

C6/G   G   D/G

feel you, to need you; there's noth - ing to keep us a -

C6/G   C/D   G   D/G

part.

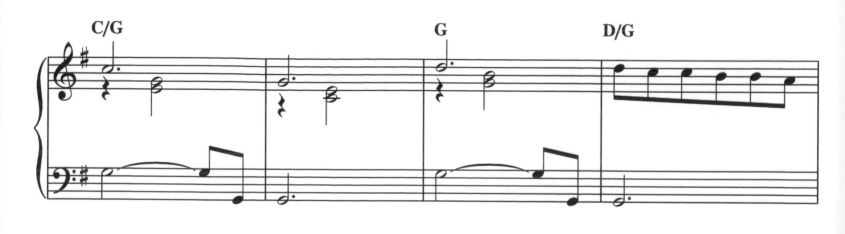

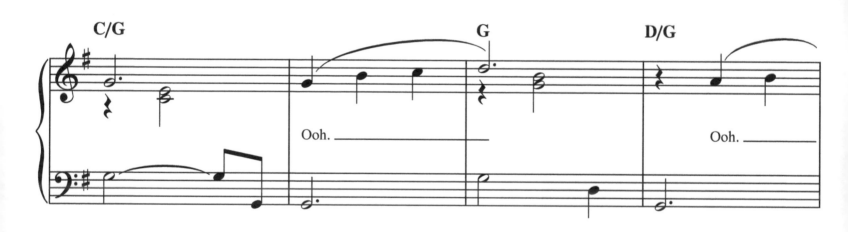

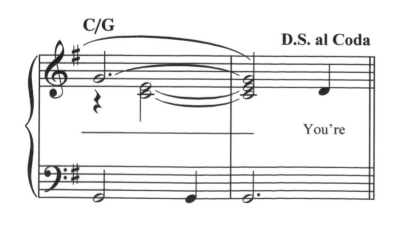

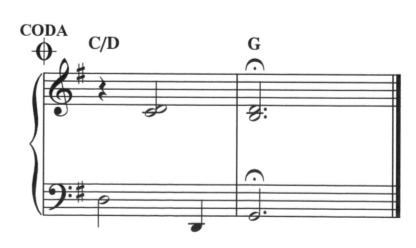

WHAT'D I SAY

Words and Music by
RAY CHARLES

170

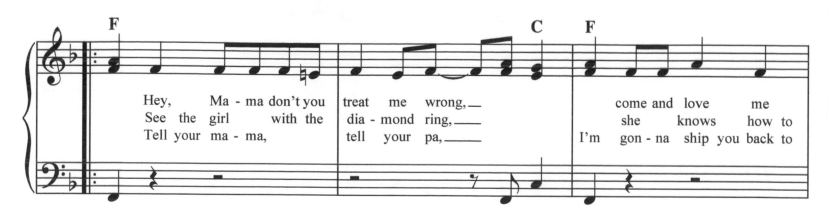

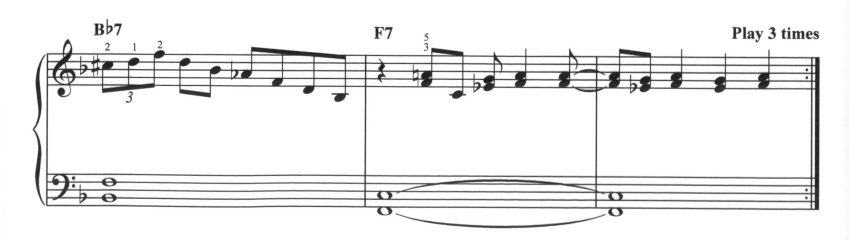

Hey, _____ (hey) _____ ho, _____ (ho) _____
Hey, _____ (hey) _____ ho, _____ (ho) _____
Huh, _____ (huh) _____ ho, _____ (ho) _____

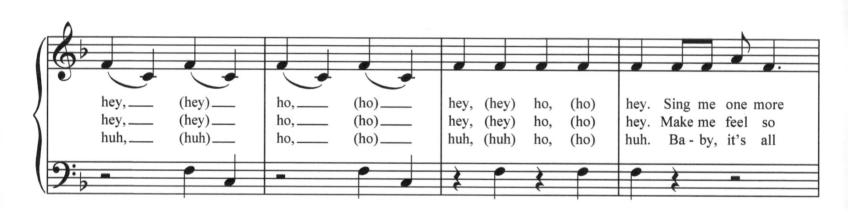

hey, _____ (hey) _____ ho, _____ (ho) _____ hey, (hey) ho, (ho) hey. Sing me one more
hey, _____ (hey) _____ ho, _____ (ho) _____ hey, (hey) ho, (ho) hey. Make me feel so
huh, _____ (huh) _____ ho, _____ (ho) _____ huh, (huh) ho, (ho) huh. Ba - by, it's all

time. Sing me one more time. Sing me one more
good. Make me feel so good. Make me feel so
right. Ba - by, it's all right, right now. Ba - by, it's all

Bb7   F

time. ___ Sing me one more time. Sing me one more
good right now. Make me feel so good. Make me feel so
right. ___ Ba - by, it's all right. Ba - by, it's all

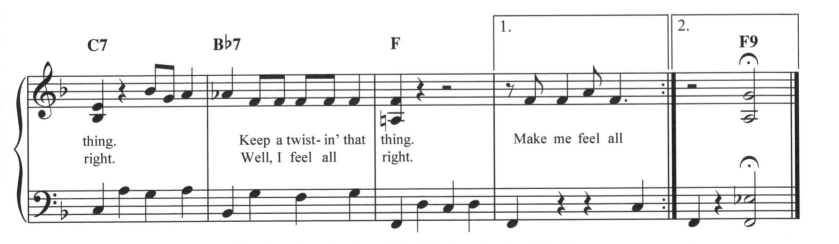

WALK ON BY

Lyric by HAL DAVID
Music by BURT BACHARACH

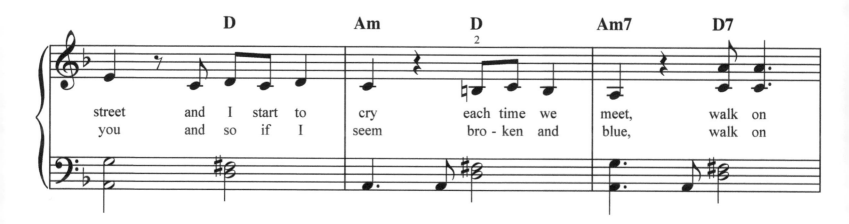

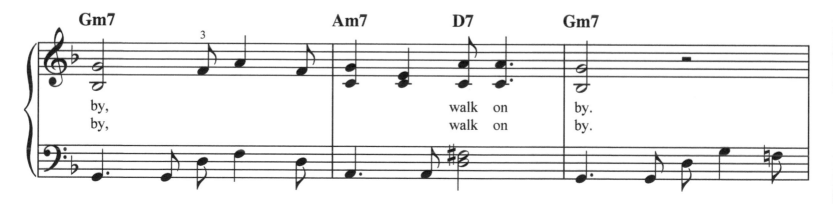

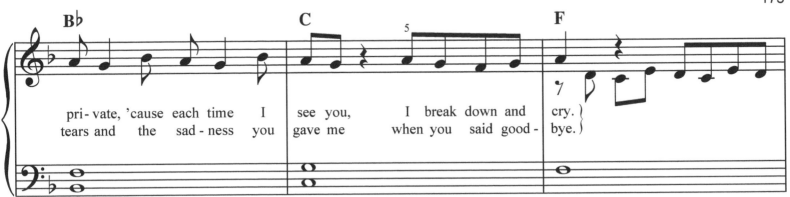

WHAT'S GOING ON

Words and Music by RENALDO BENSON,
ALFRED CLEVELAND and MARVIN GAYE

Moderately

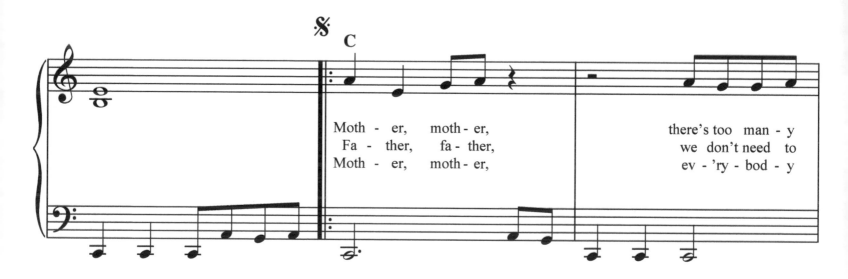

Moth - er, moth - er,
Fa - ther, fa - ther,
Moth - er, moth - er,

there's too man - y
we don't need to
ev - 'ry - bod - y

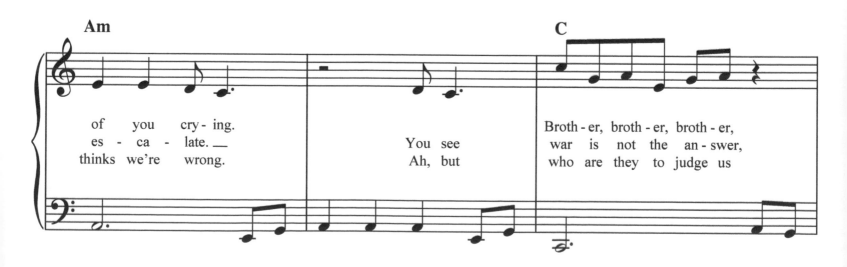

of you cry - ing.
es - ca - late. __
thinks we're wrong.

You see
Ah, but

Broth - er, broth - er, broth - er,
war is not the an - swer,
who are they to judge us

Am

there's far too man - y of you dy - ing. You __ know we've
for on - ly love can con - quer hate. _____ You __ know we've
sim - ply 'cause our hair is long. _____ Ah, you know we've

Dm7

got to find a way to bring some
got to find a way to bring some
got to find a way to bring some un - der-

1.
Dm7/G

lov - in' here to - day, __

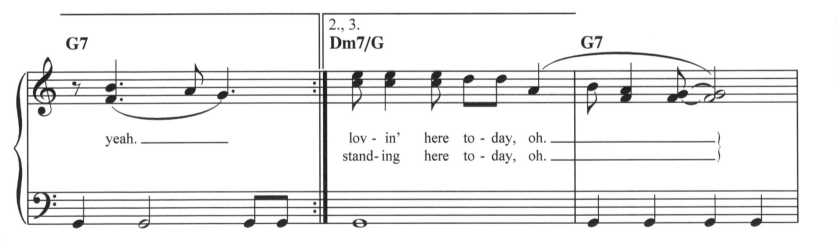

G7

yeah. _____

2., 3.
Dm7/G

lov - in' here to - day, oh. _____
stand - ing here to - day, oh. _____

G7

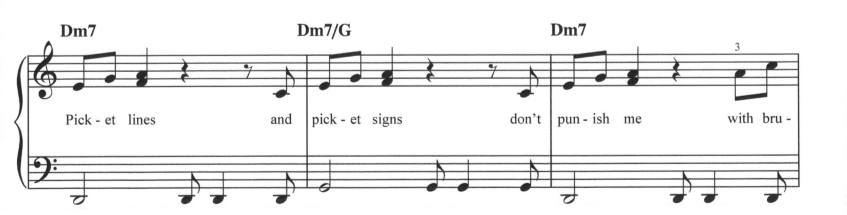

Dm7

Pick - et lines and

Dm7/G

pick - et signs don't

Dm7

pun - ish me with bru -

3

I, yi, yi, yi, yi, yi, ya, ya, ya, ya, ya. —

F/G

Be, doot, de doot; be, be, be, doot; be be, be, doot;

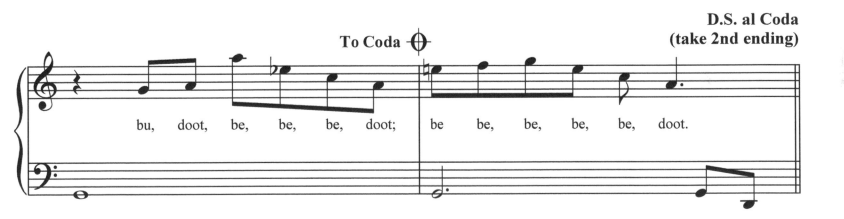

To Coda ⊕   **D.S. al Coda**
(take 2nd ending)

bu, doot, be, be, be, doot; be be, be, be, be, doot.

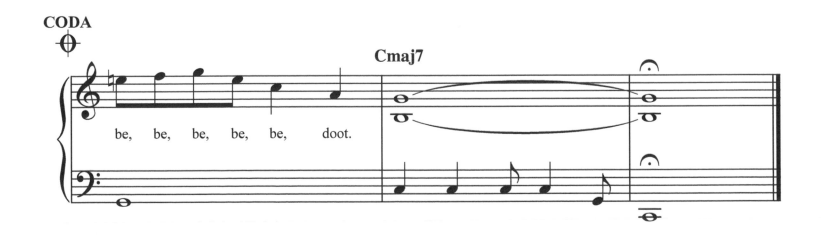

CODA

Cmaj7

be, be, be, be, be, doot.

WHAT'S LOVE GOT TO DO WITH IT

Words and Music by GRAHAM LYLE
and TERRY BRITTEN

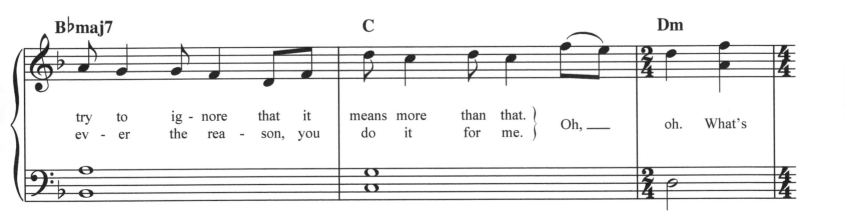

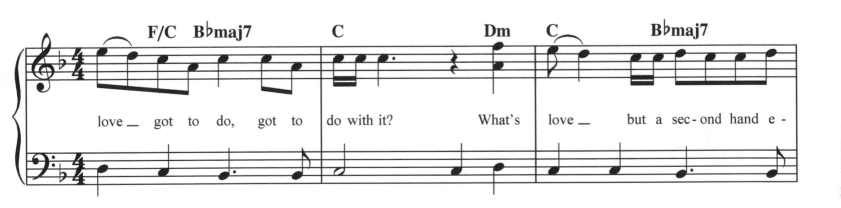

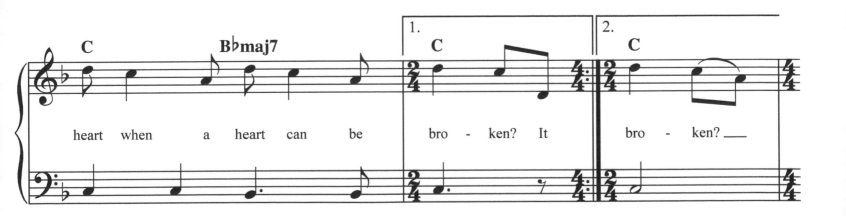

Oh,   oh. _____   I've been tak - ing on a

new di - rec - tion,   but I have _ to say, _____

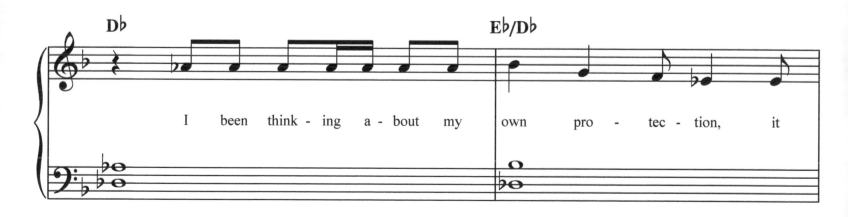

I been think - ing a - bout my own pro - tec - tion, it

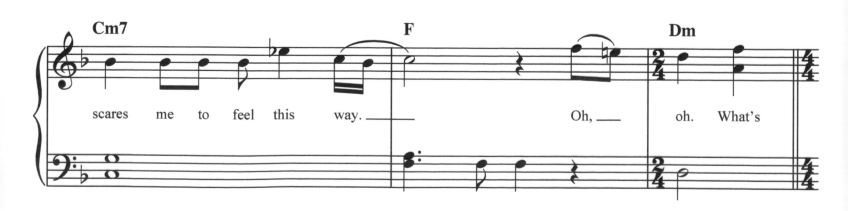

scares me to feel this way. _____   Oh, ___ oh. What's

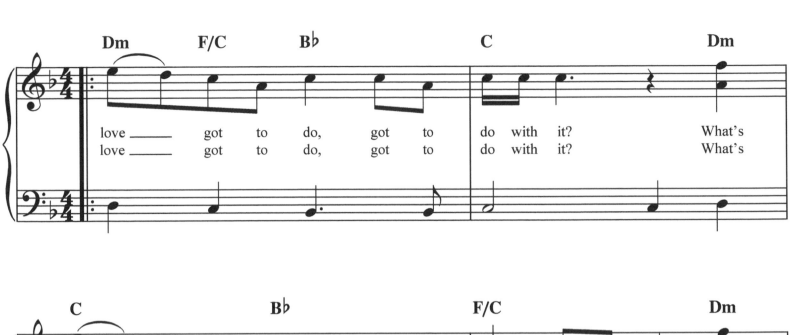

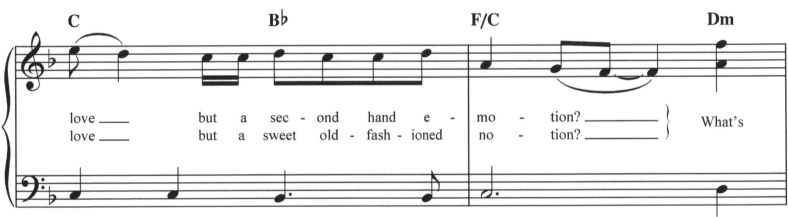

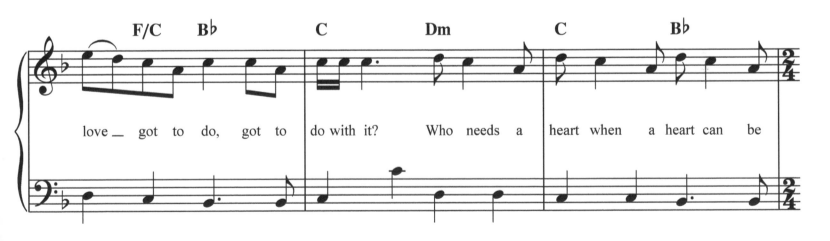

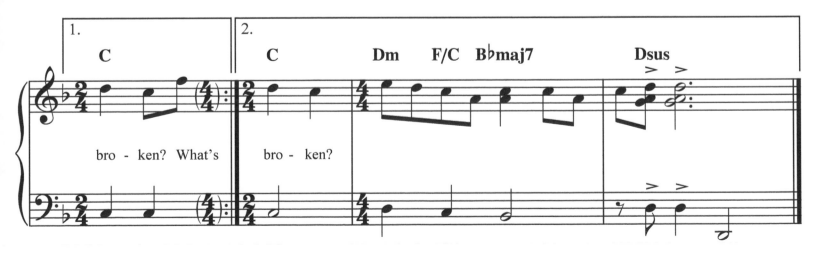

WHEN A MAN LOVES A WOMAN

Words and Music by CALVIN LEWIS
and ANDREW WRIGHT

He'd trade the world for a good thing he's found.
try - ing to hold on to what he needs.

If she is bad, _____ he can't see it. _____
He'd give up all _____ his com - forts, _____

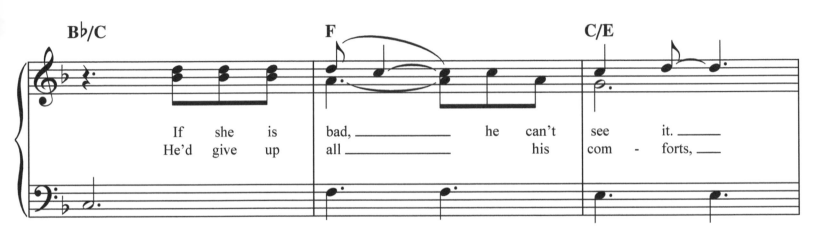

She can do _____ no wrong.
and sleep out in the rain,

Turn his back on his
if she said that's the

1.

best friend _____ if he puts her down. _____

When a

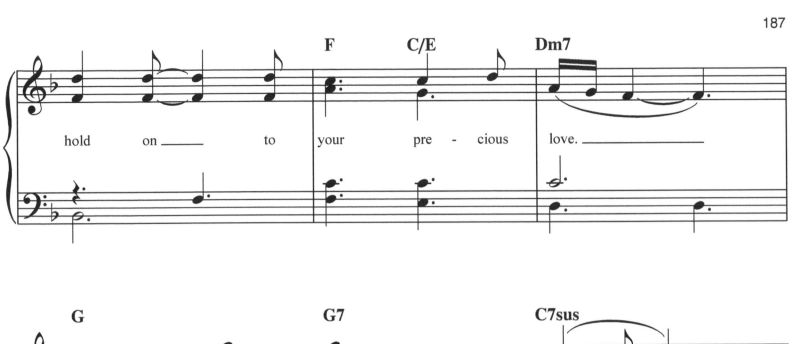

hold on _____ to your pre - cious love. _____

Ba - by, ba - by, please don't treat me bad. _____

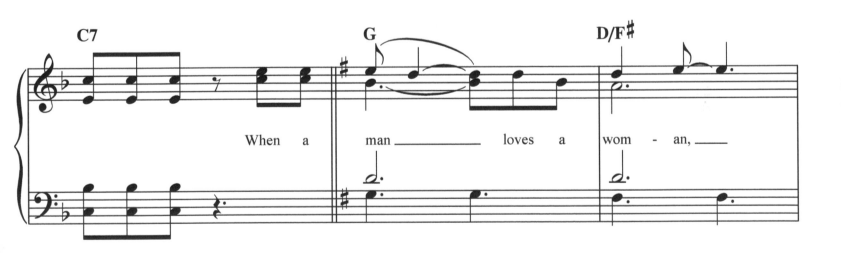

When a man _____ loves a wom - an, _____

deep down in his soul, _____ she can

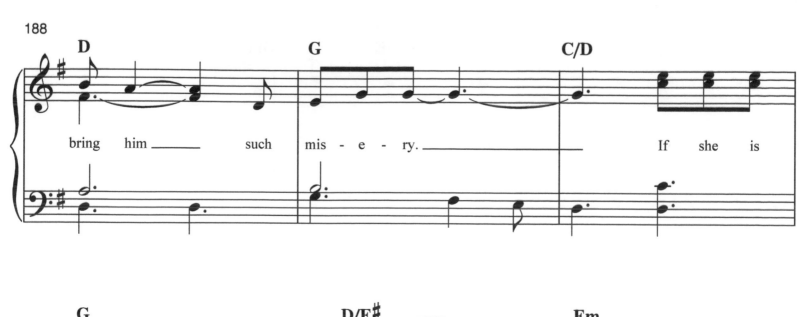

bring him _____ such mis - e - ry. _____ If she is

play - ing him for a fool, _____ he's the

last one to know. Lov - ing eyes can nev - er

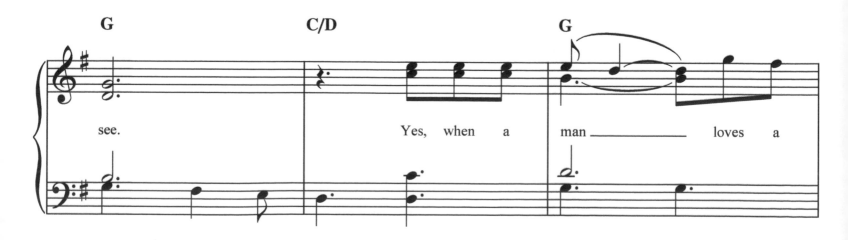

see. Yes, when a man _____ loves a

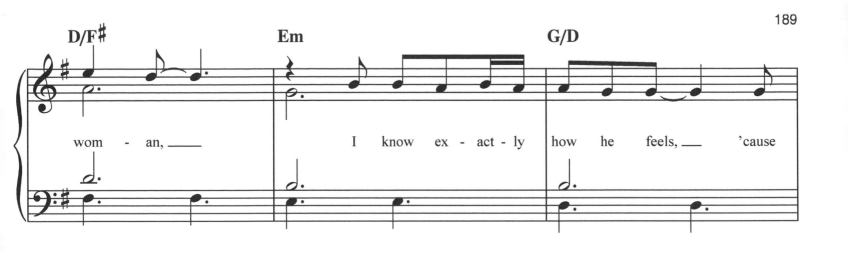

wom - an, _____ I know ex - act - ly how he feels, _____ 'cause

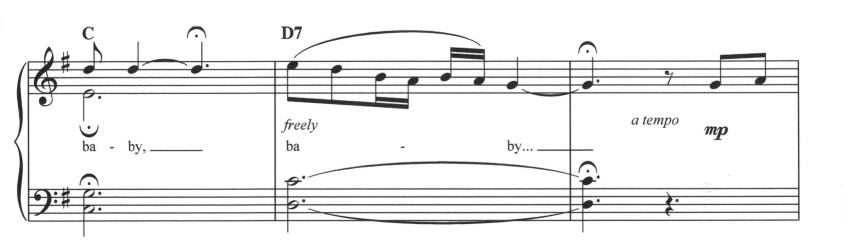

ba - by, _____ ba - by... _____ freely a tempo mp

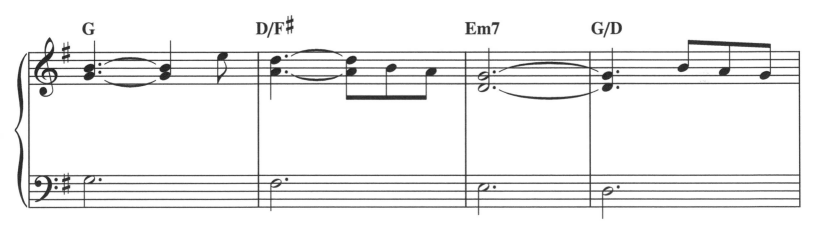

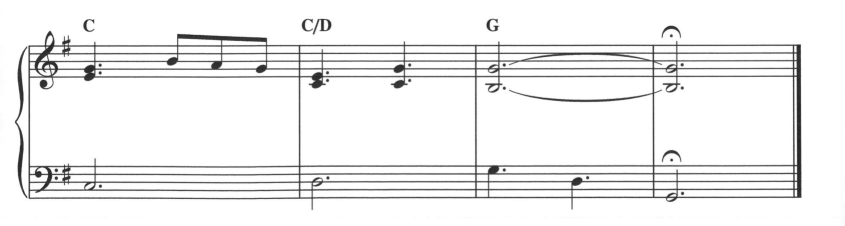

YOU CAN'T HURRY LOVE

Words and Music by EDWARD HOLLAND JR.,
LAMONT DOZIER and BRIAN HOLLAND

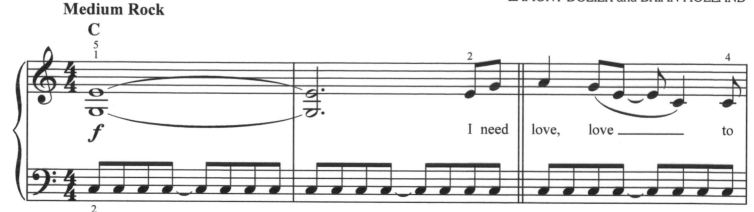

Csus   C6   F   C   To Coda

can't hur - ry love, ___ no, you'll just have to wait." ___ She said,

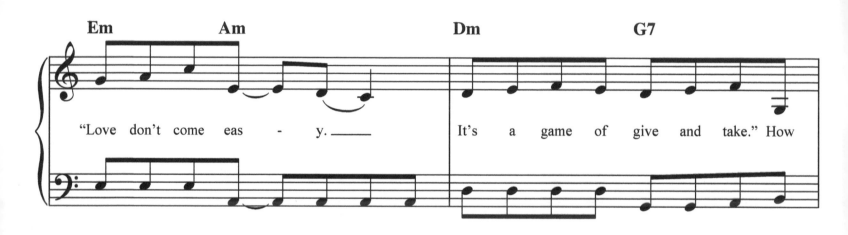

Em   Am   Dm   G7

"Love don't come eas - y. ___ It's a game of give and take." How

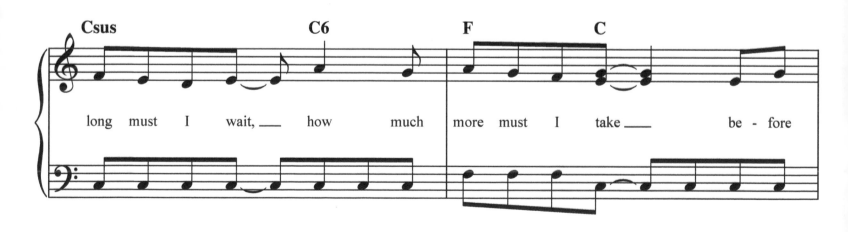

Csus   C6   F   C

long must I wait, ___ how much more must I take ___ be - fore

Em   Am   Dm   G   D.S. al Coda

lone - li - ness ___ will cause my heart, heart to break? No

193

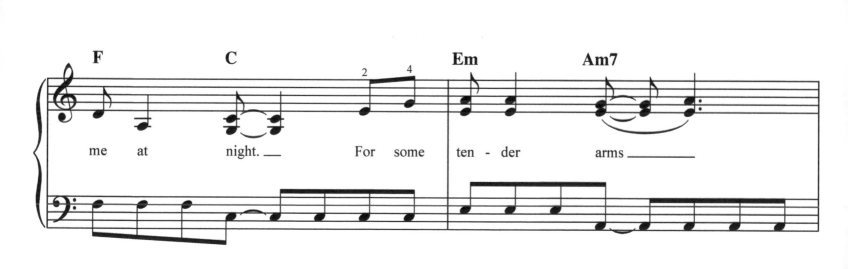

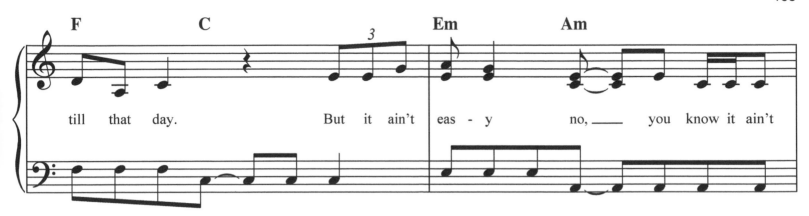

till that day.   But it ain't   eas - y   no, ____   you know it ain't

eas - y.   My ma - ma said, "You   can't hur - ry   love, __   no,   you'll

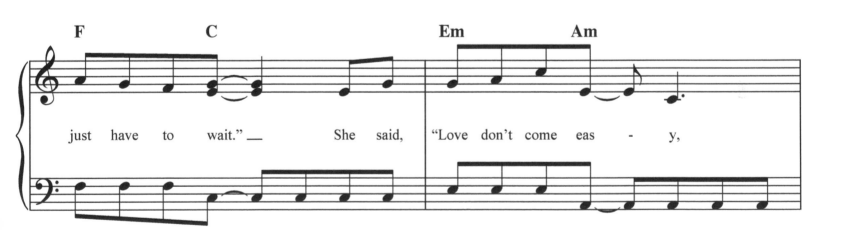

just have to wait." __   She said,   "Love don't come eas - y,

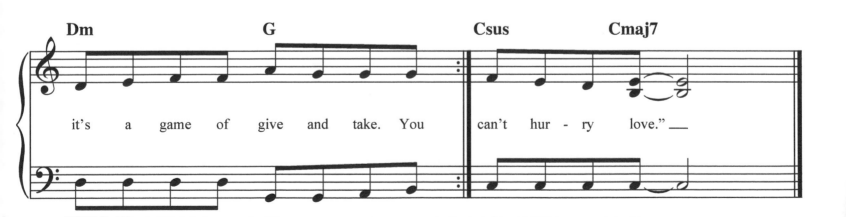

it's   a   game of give and take. You   can't hur - ry   love." __

YOU SEND ME

Words and Music by
SAM COOKE

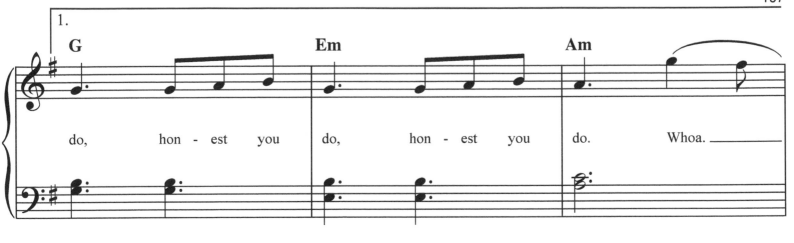

do, hon - est you do, hon - est you do. Whoa. ___

___ do, hon - est you do, hon - est you

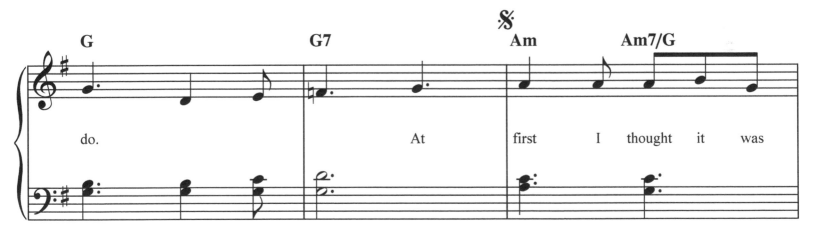

do. At first I thought it was

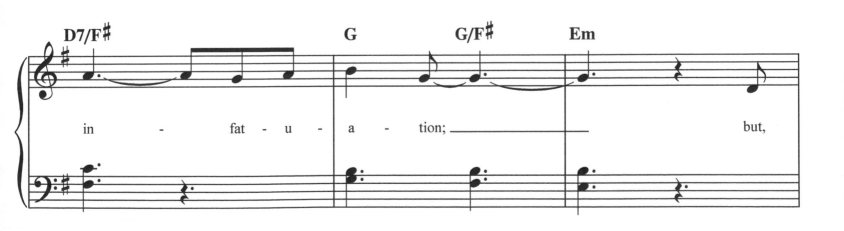

in - fat - u - a - tion; ___ but,

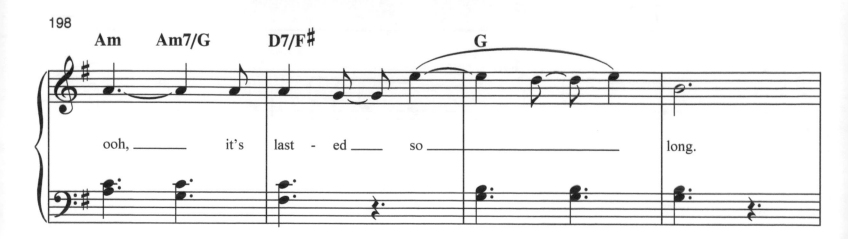

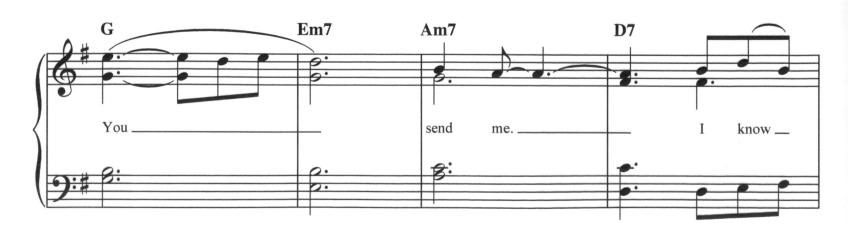

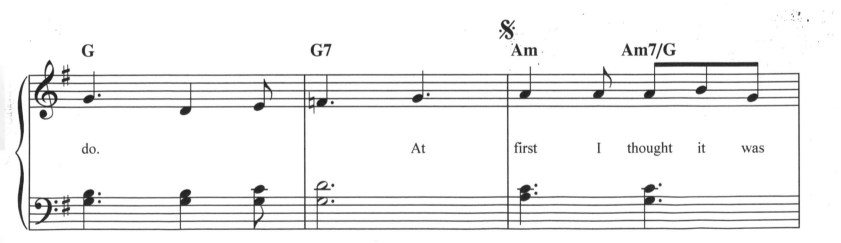

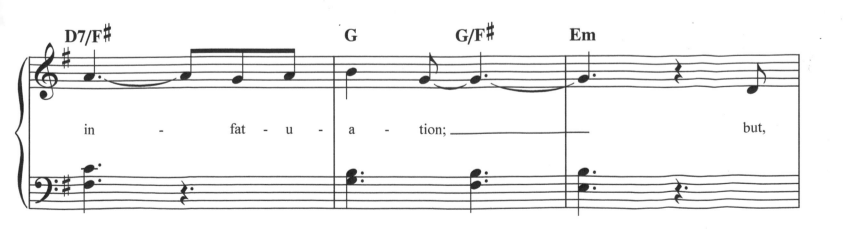

ooh, _____ it's last - ed _____ so _____ long.

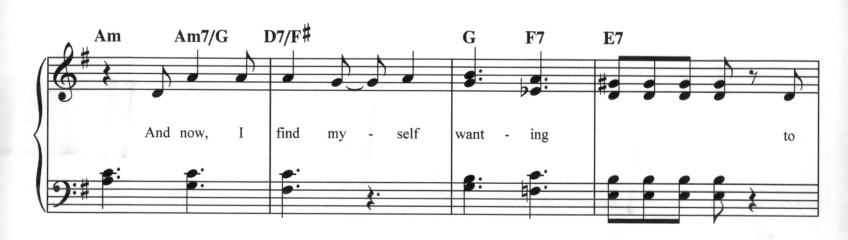

And now, I find my - self want - ing to

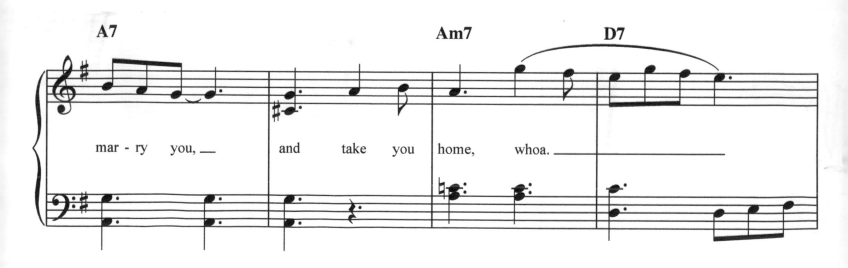

mar - ry you, ___ and take you home, whoa. _____

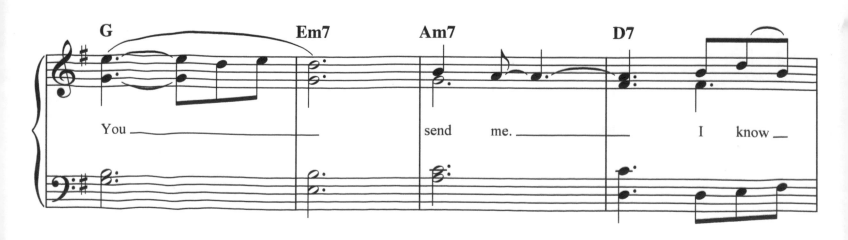

You _____ send me. _____ I know __

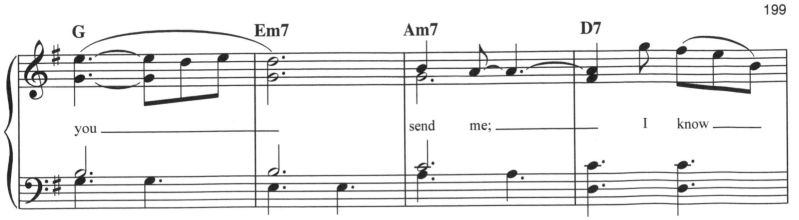

you _____ send me; _____ I know _____

you _____ send me; _____ hon - est you

To Coda

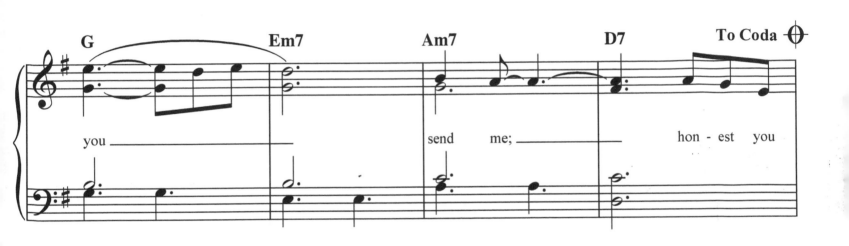

D.S. al Coda

do, hon - est you do, hon - est you do. At

CODA

do, hon - est you do, hon - est you do.
rit.

FIRST 50 SONGS
YOU SHOULD PLAY ON THE PIANO

You've been taking lessons, you've got a few chords under your belt, and you're ready to buy a songbook.
Now what? Hal Leonard has the answers in its **First 50** series.

These books contain easy to intermediate arrangements with lyrics for must-know songs.
Each arrangement is simple and streamlined, yet still captures the essence of the tune.

3-Chord Songs
00249666..............................$16.99

4-Chord Songs
00249562..............................$16.99

Acoustic Songs
00293416..............................$16.99

Baroque Pieces
00291453..............................$14.99

Blues Songs
00150167..............................$14.99

Broadway Songs
00150167..............................$14.99

Christmas Carols
00147216..............................$14.99

Christmas Songs
00172041..............................$14.99

Classical Pieces
00131436..............................$14.99

Country Songs
00150166..............................$14.99

Disney Songs
00274938..............................$19.99

Duets
00276571..............................$19.99

Early Rock Songs
00160570..............................$14.99

Folk Songs
00235867..............................$14.99

Gospel Songs
00282526..............................$14.99

Hymns
00275199..............................$14.99

Jazz Standards
00196269..............................$14.99

Kids' Songs
00196071..............................$14.99

Latin Songs
00248747..............................$16.99

Movie Songs
00150165..............................$16.99

Movie Themes
00278368..............................$16.99

Pop Ballads
00248987..............................$16.99

Pop Hits
00234374..............................$16.99

Popular Songs
00131140..............................$16.99

R&B Songs
00196028..............................$14.99

Relaxing Songs
00327506 ....$16.99

Rock Songs
00195619..............................$16.99

TV Themes
00294319..............................$14.99

Worship Songs
00287138..............................$16.99

HAL•LEONARD®

www.halleonard.com

*Prices, content and availability subject to
change without notice.*